Emotional Hustle

Release the emotional baggage and
live the life you truly deserve!

By Julie Perrigo

The Emotional Hustle

ISBN: 978-1-0682622-0-3

This book is a work of nonfiction and is based on the author's personal experiences and perspectives. To protect the privacy of individuals, some names, identifying details, and circumstances have been changed

Published in the United Kingdom with the assistance of TAUK Publishing

To my beautiful nieces and daughter-in-law. I hope, between the pages of this book, you find answers to the mystery of this great life of ours. Life can be truly amazing when we let go of our fears and learn to embrace it.

Contents

Prologue

Here I am, a mindfulness coach, and all I see on social media are posts for more coaching. It's the job of the algorithm to mathematically connect me to like-minded people, but in reality, I just get to see what every other coach on the planet is up to. It can be exhausting, and it's something I have to watch carefully to avoid spinning off into a self-destructive cycle of 'not good enough'.

It powers my cynicism like nothing else, and I recently saw a post claiming that you could achieve twelve years of transformation in just twelve minutes. It was on Facebook, so it must be true. My ego was wounded. I mean, what the hell am I doing messing around with a degree in mindfulness when I could have conquered it all in twelve minutes? Before I dismiss this claim as completely unfounded, I believe that instant mental shifts are possible. This is the entire premise of Neuro Linguistic Programming (NLP). With the right tools and support, we can shift our perspective in an instant, and when we do, there's no going back. We do experience transformation.

Yet my own experience of this process is that it's a longer road that has many twists and turns along the way. Sometimes, like with NLP shifts, we experience those eureka moments and gather momentum, much like running downhill. Other times, it seems that as we remove one barrier, it's instantly replaced by something new. So why would we bother to start on this road of personal transformation? Isn't it just the latest buzzword?

I think it runs a bit deeper than the latest fad. There is nothing more interesting than the human emotional journey, and when given the opportunity, most of us are fascinated by it. Whether we recognise it or not, every single hour of each day, we wrestle with our inner world of emotions. Whilst the Romans sat people-watching in their arenas, we watch *The Traitors* and *Love Island*. Human behaviour is relatable and tribal. On some level, it gives us an indication of where we consider ourselves to be in the pecking order of life.

We observe and judge the behaviour we align with and the actions we wouldn't condone under any circumstances. Often, we do this objectively, forgetting that, in the words of neuroscientist Damasio (2000), *'We are not thinking machines that feel; rather, we are feeling machines that think.'* According to psychiatrist and spiritual teacher Hawkins (2013), we're not just driven by our emotions, we're at their mercy. We've witnessed great advances and inventions over our lifetime, but emotionally, we haven't come far in the last 2,000 years. We only need to look at the divisive nature of the Covid-19 vaccination to understand that it doesn't take much to pitch human beings against each other. Behind the curtains of the semi-detached house adorned with the Jo Malone candles, we are still survivors at heart.

Children are fascinated by the very nature of our existence here on Earth, and as you'll discover in this book, this truly is a miracle. I smiled while listening to a recent talk from psychologist and philosopher Dr Wayne Dyer (2024). He said that he finds it extraordinary that a developing foetus has its wisdom teeth already plumbed in and ready to go. He observes that when we experience the miracle of human life, we instantly turn our back on nature with a sort of 'I'll take it from here' attitude.

His observation and the fictional writing of Dan Brown (2018) make me wonder if the human race has reached a complacency. We're assuming we've arrived at the top of our human trees, the finished articles, with nowhere else to go. Yet that very idea goes against our evolution and the adaptations we've made to survive so far. Hawkins (2013) believes that human transformation is the key to our evolution and has provided us with a roadmap, which I'll reference in this book.

Transformation feels grand or dramatic, but it's something we all experience in small ways across our lifetime. Often, it's only recognised in retrospect. We may not set an intention to transform, but when we come out of the other side, we realise that we've experienced something profound, a shift that means we can never go back to the person we were.

This is where I found myself, flapping around like a butterfly, never realising I was the caterpillar. I'm a self-confessed achiever and striver, traits that have driven me through many life-enhancing experiences. However, I recognise habits that have led me down the road of burnout and energetic exhaustion. Recently, I've noticed a shift. I was out walking in nature, pondering and reflecting on the last six years of my life, when I had an epiphany. *Oooh!* I thought to myself, *I wonder if I've transformed.* Has normal, unassuming little Julie Perrigo had an upgrade? It wasn't just about thinking differently or not kowtowing to those inner voices; I felt different, less reactive, less bothered about things.

It was more of a slow reveal than a twelve-minute euphoric transformation, but I've learnt to experience life in a completely different way, from an anxious, controlling, stressed perfectionist to a calm and less reactive sloth. There's little to observe on the outside. It's the inside that's had a complete makeover, and let's be honest, that's where most of us live, on the inside. I still have those days when I'm drowning in anxiety or self-doubt, or I feel myself going into freeze mode, feeling helplessness and resentment. I find these experiences come less and less and don't stick around for as long as they might have. When they start to become more of a permanent fixture, I'm able to take a step back to see if I'm in a relationship or an environment that's cultivating these feelings. I've seen a glimpse of a life full of boundless energy, and I'm no longer prepared to settle or waste my precious energy swimming upstream to meet the perceived expectations of society.

Day by day, I'm reclaiming my life, my emotions, my health and my energy, and at over fifty years old, it's probably about time. It's not just about building a deep sense of authentic awareness but also identifying what we leave behind or stop propping up. I've also stopped 'fixing' other people, although I still have to prevent myself from jumping in and offering unsolicited help. The urge to fix others often comes from a need to take away the suffering of others, particularly when it's something we've experienced ourselves, but it's one of those traits that can lead to resentment when the person we are helping isn't as grateful as we think they should be. Maybe they decide they have the answers all along or ask someone else. None of that is our concern, as we can only take responsibility for our own actions. Herein lies one of the attractions of fixing because when we offer to solve someone else's problems, we have flexible accountability. It seems far easier to step into their world and offer direction than it does to look closer to home and do our own work. When we explore our inner work, we realise how much facing our own challenges helps us grow, so who are we to take that opportunity away from someone else?

We can always offer support on mutual terms if we're able to avoid fixing someone else's life by trying to align it with our own view of the world. This approach is founded on an underlying assumption that their version of happiness aligns with ours.

So doing our own exploration is about building that awareness of our traits and habits. We begin to let go of the ideals that weigh us down, and when we enjoy travelling light, we learn what we can leave behind. Understanding boundaries and responsibilities can be simple stuff, yet very powerful when we get it right. We can spend an entire lifetime trying to shift our emotional baggage, but what if we learnt to avoid picking it up in the first place?

I pass on this advice after getting most of it wrong for half a century. Here in this book, I lay it all out for you just to illustrate that we can all exorcise our demons. I highlight the emotional weights we carry and the roadmap and skills for moving towards an authentic life. So, here's your first fork in the road.

If you're looking for a quick fix, then there's a great twelve-minute transformation available on social media. If you're ready to go a little deeper, then I invite you to join me on a road that took me fifty years to navigate. *The Emotional Hustle* maps the rollercoaster of our emotional landscape because transformation is more like a game of snakes and ladders than a linear path. Just when we think we've conquered our mountain, life throws us a curveball, and we feel like we're back at the start. Yet we never go back to where we started. We're always a little bit further along the road.

I invite you to open your heart and mind and to see where it leads. Have faith in the process because after years of searching for answers, I fell into my own inner work completely by accident and yet it still worked. All you need to do is keep showing up and following the guidance within.

Welcome to *The Emotional Hustle.*

Part One

Introduction

It was about 6am on a cold September morning in 2017. I was huddled up on the couch in the corner of a draughty 1960s conservatory. It was long and narrow and had been used by the previous owners as a space for relaxation and a utility room. In my opinion, these two things did not go together. That said, we had turned the space into chaos. It was packed to the walls with oversized furniture. We were living on a building site, and every corner was stuffed to the brim as we unsuccessfully attempted to squash our belongings into a smaller house. I'd turned into one of these people on *Location, Location, Location,* who claim they want to downsize to a four-acre farmhouse with six bedrooms and grounds for Alpacas. Here we were trying to squash twenty years of history into a smaller space. Furniture that was lost in our sprawling Edwardian semi, with sixteen-foot rooms and high ceilings, was now stacked and positioned at odd angles whilst we rewired and remodelled. I didn't feel like we were winning, particularly as our old wooden dining room table, which we'd deconstructed to fit in the greenhouse, was beginning to show signs of decay. I knew how it felt.

Our rude, oversized, vocal and aloof tabby cat, Tiggy, was extremely disappointed with the impact of our life choices. It was clear she held us in contempt, yet at seventeen years old, I suspected we'd done a few things right. She had the opportunity to come and go as she pleased and hadn't, to my knowledge, had a better offer. The house was a traditional semi with a dining room at the back and a living room at the front. At some point in the past, the dividing wall between the two rooms had been knocked through to form a single room and the tired, old, pink carpet that had covered this floor had been removed to check for tile adhesive asbestos. The carpet now lay in a crumpled, damp heap in the garden. Skip day was imminent! We were going to rebuild the dividing wall, but for now, we had placed our couches on either side of the space. Tiggy had made her new home here on the cold, tiled floor, in the gap we'd created with the couches. We didn't move her to a more comfortable place; instead, we found a fleecy blanket for her to lie on. Unfortunately, as the dividing wall began to rise, poor Tiggy was moving home again, and her route to the door and, more importantly, her food was changing every few days. As this wall went up, others came down, and doorways moved. As cat retirement goes, this was most unsatisfactory.

As I sit here writing this chapter on a remote island off the coast of West Scotland, it occurs to me that this scene should open the book. It wasn't an image I ever intended to include, as I'm very much a cut-to-the-chase sort of person, but I realised that this chaotic, cluttered scene bears no comparison to what we might imagine as the starting point for a profound life-changing transformation.

Perhaps we imagine it comes with a huge signpost, saying 'Start here' or 'Perfect spiritual conditions ahead'. Mine began with a disgruntled cat, a house full of chaos and a book recommendation from a friend. It was amongst this chaos that a series of life-changing events began.

The book that seemed to start everything led me to an inner discovery that would free me from a forty-five-year struggle with happiness, stress and the ability to just be content. Whilst we all have survival instincts that can be wired towards negativity, mine had tipped a little too far in this direction and from around three years of age, I'd developed a protective mistrust of other people. I'm in absolute awe of those who love to meet new people because I have only known fear and apprehension. My fierce sense of independence has created an emotional shield, but this withdrawal could not protect me from narcissistic relationships or childhood bullying. We talk a lot in mindfulness about distraction; mine was striving and achieving. A lovely cycle of being busy and having the outward trappings of success, none of which could prop up my sense of self-worth.

In my early twenties, I began to find my rhythm, and my inner confidence started to grow, but sadly, this was completely shattered by the sudden death of my mother. Her death left a massive gap in my life, particularly as we were just starting to become friends. As I grew older, I came to really appreciate the strong, resilient woman who had taught me everything I know about survival. That's how I lived my life, with the ability to armour up on the outside whilst struggling with anxiety on the inside. Anxiety wasn't something I recognised at the time because, like many people who live life with an underlying sense of fear, these feelings are part of our normal existence. I had no inclination that there was any other way to live, no inclination that I had true choices over how to feel or experience the richness of life. I had no aspirations to truly thrive because I thought everything was okay until it wasn't.

Keeping everything together on the inside eventually impacted my physical and mental health, and I was diagnosed with work-related stress and depression. What initially seemed to be a single episode started to become a pattern. It happened enough times for me to stop looking at the outside world and start looking closer to home. In a desperate attempt to fix myself, I explored many options, including counselling, neuro-linguistic programming, leadership courses and life coaching. Each programme gave me a small piece of the puzzle, but I still felt there was something missing until, eventually, I found the answers I was looking for. This is when the world started to make sense.

When I started studying and practising mindfulness, I had absolutely no idea what it was and yet, even with no intention to make the life changes I so needed to make, I began to uncover the means to unpack all of the gremlins. I came to understand the true power of the fear response and its impact on the body. I recognised the personality traits that would lead me down the same road to stress again and again. I learnt about the nervous system, and just as I thought I had a grasp on humanity, I came across the energy map from Dr David Hawkins.

It was here that I truly began to consider human energy. I'd experienced interrupting the stress management system and building an authentic emotional resilience, but I still struggled with the fluctuation in my energy levels.

In scientific terms, energy is always linked to calories, and I appreciate that exercise influences our energy levels. Yet I also know that two days are never energetically alike, and if I developed the perfect nutritional formula for high energy, I could still feel different each day. I couldn't quite form my ideas around energy, which is why the discovery of Hawkins' (2013) emotional scale came at just the right time. As the author of *Power versus Force* and *Transcending the Levels of Consciousness,* you may assume that the work of Hawkins is founded in faith and beliefs, but he's a scientist, philosopher and psychiatrist. Dr Hawkins appreciates the scientific world, the holistic world and the spiritual world. His thought-provoking work maps our emotional journey from the debilitating feelings of shame right up to the elusive inner peace we all seek. Describing emotion as 'Energy in **motion',** Hawkins connects our emotions and energy differently. It transcends the intake of calories that we have come to solely link to energetic input. This concept is understood in Eastern traditions such as Reiki, a practice that balances and unblocks the flow of energy within the body. Yet, it remains relatively unexplored and can even be perceived as irrelevant or unproven in Western science. For me, this is the joy of the times in which we are now living: a unique period in history where Western scientific research finally has the tools to uncover what has been known and understood within Eastern traditions for many centuries. Our scientific logic is being challenged as the fields of quantum physics and neuroscience bump into the traditional approaches of Reiki and mindfulness. Whilst Reiki can balance our energy flows, the emotional energy scale provides us with context or a roadmap. It sounds easy, doesn't it?

The challenge is that knowledge isn't enough. We imagine we have emotional control, but we don't. This is not a criticism; it's linked to the way our human brain operates. It's very powerful and thinking or solving problems takes a lot of energy, so the brain learns techniques, stores them and then re-uses them to take shortcuts. When we react to a situation or resolve an issue, the brain stores the answers. The next time we experience something similar, we don't work it out all over again. We re-run our pre-packed response. This isn't problematic as an approach as long as we're aware that most of our solutions are developed emotionally before the executive part of our brain is fully functional. They form neural pathways and connections in the brain. Each time we respond in a particular way, the associated neural pathways get thicker and stronger until they are available as automatic reactions. When we are travelling to a new place, we follow a set of instructions. It can take just three or four trips before we start to recognise the signposts and follow the route without guidance. This is how our automatic responses begin to form.

To transcend our early embedded wiring, it's necessary to bring some of our long-term solutions out into the open where we can assess their suitability. This requires interrupting these automated patterns, a technique that can be developed through mindfulness. These pathways were created emotionally, so it's the awareness of the body that builds a knowledge of our inner landscape, giving us the foundations to move towards the sense of inner freedom that we all desire.

Energy, emotions and mindfulness—this is the journey of *The Emotional Hustle.* Recognising the traits and thoughts that keep us trapped whilst creating new habits that will empower us to return to a place of inner contentment. In this book, I weave an emotional path through my own experience, starting with the debilitating emotions that weigh more heavily on us. As you follow, some of my experiences will resonate deeply and might provoke a strong reaction. This is usually an indication that there's something to explore. I'll provide tools, practices and reflections along the way. Hopefully, these will help you to shift some of the emotional weight that is draining your energy.

If I had one life lesson to offer before we start, it's that we cannot outrun or out-achieve our emotional baggage. Until we learn to clear it out and let it go, we get to carry it everywhere, whether we realise it or not.

Whatever our challenges, we can take inspiration from the spiritual traditions of the Lotus Flower. It grows and thrives in the mud, and yet it's a symbol of purity. Each day, it rises from the mud to open and bloom. Without the mud, there's no lotus flower, and I have a lot of mud to share with you.

Shame and Glory

It was quite by accident that during my forties, I discovered some rather intriguing personal insights. It wasn't the sort of insight one discovers on a retreat in Torquay '*...with herds of wildebeests sweeping majestically across the plain,*' Cleese & Booth (1997). Instead, it was light and entertaining. Nevertheless, it made me curious about how different life might have been had I discovered these gems of insight a little sooner.

I had been invited to Ladies Day at Aintree Racecourse. Despite the insinuation that a certain standing in society is required in order to attend such an event, it turns out that a nice dress and a sober look will suffice. Oh and of course, a ticket. Being completely new to the experience, I had no expectations of the day, but it wasn't too long before disappointment started to set in. There I was, trussed up in my black and white strapless size twelve dress, toddling around in a pair of black peep-toe heels adorned with a dainty bow. At this point in my writing, I feel I must pause for a moment to pay tribute to the pre-menopausal body that could squeeze itself into a size twelve. Within a couple of hours, we found ourselves wading through discarded stinky beer bottles, having flashbacks to the sort of nightclubs that only became full when everywhere else was closed. The ones with the sticky carpets and suspiciously wet loo floors. We were in the standing pen, and to make matters worse, my horse-choosing skills were equally awful. Bidding on all seven races, there was just one on which we didn't lose money, race number six. In fact, race number six became the backdrop to my remarkable little self-discovery.

My lovely friend Clare will not mind me saying that she is always up for some food, and it was during race number six that we decided to throw caution to the wind and gamble our betting stake on sausage and chips. We still chose our horses, and when true to form, they lost, we revelled in our success, far from disappointed, as we reached out our hands to receive our true winnings—sausage and chips twice. Almost immediately, our excitement was dimmed as the flaw in our plan began to dawn. There were no tables in this area. As I stared down at my two hands, I knew I needed both to eat my food, but one was already occupied with a full bottle of Budweiser.

Now, in parts of this book, I will discuss core beliefs and how they're formed from consensus reality. These unchallenged truths can set in when everyone around us has the same belief or opinion. Within our family DNA, there's a golden rule that we never waste beer. So here was my dilemma: where could I store my Budweiser whilst I tucked into my takeaway? As I gazed around, I realised that the obvious answer was some sort of third hand and one that wouldn't come from my friend, who was tucking in as I pondered.

It was at this moment that my amazing insight came to me. Yes, at the age of forty-two, the number we already know to be the meaning of life, I discovered that I could hold a bottle of beer in my cleavage! I was absolutely delighted with the discovery and quickly realised that the skill also seemed to make me more attractive to the opposite sex. As with any new discovery, we always wonder how life might have turned out had we been equipped with this knowledge sooner. I was sure that I could have put this skill to great use in my twenties. However, regrets aside, I rested the beer in its new home as I tucked into sausage and chips, secure in the knowledge that race number six had by far been the most successful race of the day.

When I drink alcohol, I feel there's a moment in the cycle of drinking. It's an easing of the pressures of life or the gentle release of those inhibitions that sometimes keep us in check but at other times hold us back. In this moment, we feel free to be just as we are and when we recognise this experience, we want so desperately for those sensations to hang around. This is a form of being in the moment and being happy as we are. Maybe the mind settles a little and stops struggling with those impossible expectations. Maybe for a few minutes, the endless to-do list stops cycling around. A rational mind might recognise this sense of feeling settled and stay with those sensations. The not-so-sober mind clings to this experience of bliss by drinking even more alcohol. I've observed this thought process in myself and recognise it as the turning point. It's the door to the hangover and everything leading up to it. Once we go beyond this point, there is very little to be done to turn back the clock. It was on such an occasion that I made another unfortunate discovery.

On turning forty, I was sitting in the hair salon chair with root stain on my head, staring into a ready-mixed cappuccino. Realising it was my birthday, my hairdresser kindly offered me a free celebratory haircut whilst inviting herself along to my party. I'd planned the event for several years when the bank I'd worked for hired a party boat on the River Dee, Chester. So, a few hours later, prosecco in hand, there we were boating up the Dee. It was a memorable evening, and having always hung around with musicians or computer geeks, I really was quite flattered that my hairdresser and her partner, a couple who referred to their own home as Beckingham Palace, thought my party was stylish enough to attend. A few months later, we found ourselves invited to their home to celebrate their new kitchen. Whilst her partner served up his version of an Ibiza club scene playlist, we gathered around a fire pit, toasting marshmallows. Whilst I don't think I'm addicted to marshmallows, I must have resembled a stuffed hamster as I continually shoved them into my mouth long after everyone else had lost interest. In between eating marshmallows and drinking red wine, my friend persuaded me to try some little green shots.

I'm really too much of a control freak to try shots. I like the slow administration of wine and having an understanding of how many glasses I can drink before it's too much. However, having a persuasive friend and being a polite guest, I did join in, and this became my first and last experience of absinthe.

I've heard horror stories of people drinking too much and choking on their vomit as they sleep. Luckily, in these situations, my body is so much more capable than my mind. Like someone possessed, my body throws itself upright halfway through my sleep, propelling me towards the bathroom where, with poltergeist force, it projects the entire contents of my stomach in the general vicinity of the toilet. The full cycle of shame is usually completed the next day when I get to locate each little soggy red morsel and clean it up. However, on this occasion, I'd gone too far. Having found myself propelled out of my bed halfway to the bathroom, it dawned on me that I wasn't going to make it. Not for the faint-hearted, this was another moment of self-realisation. It appears that even when the contents of my stomach are glued together with marshmallow, I cannot hold those contents in one hand!

So, this might not be the material you expect to read from a mindfulness teacher writing a book on personal transformation, but acknowledging our downfalls is part of our growth. It is the capacity to face our own fears that helps us to move forward, and one of the most debilitating emotions that we face is shame. When it comes to feelings of shame, there are many shades. What might be shameful to you will not bother someone else, and vice versa. How it weaves its way into our story when we experience it impacts its power over us. I'm ashamed to share that story, but for me, it's not the hardest shame story I'll share because, as an adult, I can unpick it and apply perspective. I recognise that I went too far and drank too much, but if I'm ashamed of anything, it's this behaviour or lapse in judgement. It's not who I am.

With many difficult emotions, we identify with them so fully that we believe that is who we are. Think about these two sentences. 'I feel ashamed' versus 'I experience shame'. This is the power of perspective because in the second sentence, we recognise shame as an emotion that was present for us, but just like our thoughts or the weather, it passes through. When we feel ashamed or become ashamed, it attaches to our personality, leaving us feeling stuck or unable to move forward. In our culture, we hear phrases such as 'shame on you' or 'you should be ashamed of yourself', leading to our behaviour and our sense of self becoming intertwined. Left unchecked, we can feel ashamed of who we are as a person, so we hide our true selves for fear of losing the love or friendship of those around us.

Brené Brown describes shame as the fear of disconnection because it's the sense that if we were truly seen, people would be so disgusted that they'd want nothing to do with us. It can leave us feeling so scared to be seen that we literally diminish ourselves or hide away. The debilitating nature of shame represents the lowest emotional vibration on the Hawkins scale of evolution (2013); hence, it's the starting point for our journey.

The fear that accompanies shame is visceral and existential because it's connected to centuries of human DNA when our very survival was dependent on our acceptance into a tribe. So, the fear of exclusion, linked to shame, is synonymous with death and when we link shame to our personality and not our behaviour, we may fear that we don't deserve to live.

This is the true detrimental power of shame and often the weapon of choice in narcissistic relationships. So, with any shame experience, perspective can be everything, but what about those shame stories that form before we have any perspective to offer?

In 1949, Hebb coined the phrase *'Neurons in the brain that fire together, wire together'*. With extensive studies in neuroscience and the aid of brain imaging tools, we are gaining a greater understanding of the emotional formation of the brain. Hebb's observation is that experiences that occur at the same time become intrinsically linked. In simple terms, it could be the song that takes us back to a particular day or relationship. We're able to understand these experiences, but the ones we have no memory of still have a bearing on our emotions, even though we don't recognise the source. These can be experiences that wire together during our early years. As we often seek patterns that validate our beliefs, each time these connections play out, much like a muscle, we strengthen that belief.

Our self-worth is not related to our financial abundance

We might agree with the sentence above intellectually, but this can be completely different to how we feel about it. It is the emotional attachment to an idea that unwittingly drives our belief system and our behaviour. From an early age, I developed a sense that my self-worth was defined by how much money my family had and as we didn't have much, this formed the basis of what was low self-esteem. I'm not referring to the sense of status that education teaches us to aspire to. For me, it was a deep sense of our worth as human beings, being defined by our financial status.

To unpack this process, it helps to start right at the beginning by imagining two newborn babies side by side. As we gaze at the newborns, there is no doubt in our mind that these children are equally deserving of all that life has to offer. It might be that they are born into very different lifestyles and do not have access to the same opportunities in life. However, the point is that they are both equally deserving and whether these opportunities exist or not, it does not lessen the human worth of that child.

Yet, as children, we quickly learn about the power of money, and its lack can leave us with a sense of helplessness and hopelessness. We pick up on beliefs within our household and form ideas that life is tough, money is difficult to come by, and we won't have the pleasures that others experience in life. Even when life shifts and our circumstances improve, we can be stuck with the old story, the lingering sense that, for us, things are tougher than for everyone else. The belief continues long after the evidence fades. These beliefs may start at home but can be unwittingly validated by external sources.

Whilst I often experienced unkind comments about growing up in a council flat, this childish bullying just confirmed what I already believed. I was ashamed of who I was, and it started with something as simple as a biscuit.

I wasn't in this particular school very long, and from school photographs, I know I was five or six years old when on an ordinary Monday morning, our young teacher came into class with an exciting idea. I liked this particular teacher, but now, because of her idea and the great pain it would bring, I had to change my mind and dislike her. I was a child, and it had to be one way or the other. The teacher wanted us all to bring in 2p on Thursday morning, and as a treat, we could all have a biscuit with our morning break.

As I sat in my seat, consumed with horror and dread, I searched the room for just one face. Was there one person who didn't think this was a good idea? I already knew I couldn't ask. If I asked for money, not only would Mum be annoyed, but she'd probably wonder why she was being asked to pay 2p for a single biscuit when she could probably get an entire packet from the Kwik Save for the same price. It was a ridiculous suggestion, and I certainly wasn't prepared to bear the brunt of Mum's irritation when it wasn't even my idea.

So, there I was, trapped in six-year-old hell. Each day, I weighed up the risks of asking Mum versus telling the teacher that her idea was stupid. In the past, the teacher was nice, and I might have been able to tell her the truth, but the biscuit incident had moved her firmly into enemy territory. Even if I could bring up the courage to tell her, how could I do it without the rest of the class hearing? The last thing I wanted was to be the centre of everybody's ridicule or pity. Sometimes, there were opportunities on the way to school when it was just the two of us, but when Mum seemed really happy and not stressed, I didn't want to ruin it with this question.

As the school days passed by and the biscuits weren't mentioned, I lived in hope of some form of divine intervention. Maybe there'd be an earthquake or a fire, and we'd have to evacuate. I even lived in hope that my teacher had abandoned the idea. Then on the last day before biscuit treat day, just as we were lifting our coats from the hangers, she let out her cheerful reminder to bring in our 2ps the following day.

So, more quickly and yet longer than expected, Thursday morning arrived, and despite days of worry and scheming, I had not come up with a single idea to save me from this awful dilemma. I could think of nothing else as the morning hours dragged by, my anxiety rising as the break time loomed. I was so frightened that I even considered talking to some of the other girls in the class, but they were all paired or grouped, and I didn't feel there was a single person who would understand my predicament.

As we came in from break, the seats appeared to be grouped in a U shape, with the centre of the U separated by a post. I seated myself at the end of the horseshoe nearest to the door, putting off the pain of the encounter as long as possible and yet the pain and anticipation were as grave as anything I could possibly experience—even death. I remember the extreme nature of my feelings, the unequipped mind with no capacity for the problem at hand, seeing something as extreme as death as the only escape.

It's no coincidence that the word mortified is derived from the French word for death or we have the saying 'I wanted the ground to swallow me up'. As a six-year-old girl, the only thing that stood before me and my dignity was a disaster of catastrophic proportions and as I watched the teacher move around the circle, swapping her biscuits for those 2p pieces, my throat just got drier and drier. Everyone was just joining in as if nothing was wrong. Not a single person had forgotten or opted out.

As I looked around the room, I felt like my thoughts were on show. It appeared to me that every single person in the room knew what was coming. It was like they could sense the fear in a game of chance. They were all waiting for that one person who was going to let the side down. Then, before I knew it, the teacher took a different route when she came to the post. Instead of going across the bottom of the U shape, she came back to my side to work her way down. Suddenly, she was there, five or six kids earlier than expected. I really don't know why it made such a difference. Maybe I was still hoping for that one child to break the status quo. The timing had absolutely no bearing on the outcome, but the shock and suddenness seemed to just compound my fear.

She stood in front of me, staring down expectantly, and I could think of only one option—I lied!

"I'm sorry, Miss. I forgot."

As she delivered her look of dismay and disappointment, she

pointed out that everyone had been reminded the day before. I remember wondering how she imagined that her response would somehow magic away the problem. Now, she was stuck and didn't know what to do, so she moved on and said she'd come back to me at the end. I sat quietly, eyes towards the floor, as she moved down the rest of the line. I could feel the weight of those tiny stares as I sat, and I wished for just one other person to break the promise. Surely, there was just one other person who hadn't joined in.

I could feel my eyes welling up, the tears stinging as I tried to keep them in. It wasn't just the teacher; I'd let everyone in the class down. I'd ruined the happy biscuit treat moment, and it wasn't even my fault. How was everyone going to eat their biscuit in peace with one person excluded? The tension was absolutely palpable, and then, as if from nowhere, her dilemma was solved. Sitting directly opposite me was my cousin Steven, who raised his hand and offered to pay for my biscuit. As the teacher agreed, the tension in the room was released like someone had lifted the lid from a pressure cooker.

I was relieved the ordeal was over, but I'd also been prepared to face my fate. There was some part of me that wanted to do without because there was strength in taking my punishment. This was the only way I could take any control of the situation, and was preferable to what I only imagined was the pity from the rest of the class. Yet the assumption of pity could be unfounded. When we imagine that we know the thoughts and views of others, we do them a disservice. We assume we know what they're thinking or feeling, but we can only base those assumptions on our own experience of reality. This is how connection and empathy work. We imagine the feelings of others in a particular situation.

It might be difficult for a group of five or six-year-olds to understand the complexity of lack if this experience sits outside their own reality. What they can experience is the fear of being outside of the group. Perhaps they also feel uncomfortable that without making a single decision, they find themselves included whilst someone else is not.

I felt the defensive animosity of someone placed on the outside through no fault of their own and the resentment of no choice. In this moment, I felt completely alone with no one to turn to. How could I admit to my mum that I'd hidden this from her, and why? Unfortunately, the ordeal didn't end there, as the teacher deemed the event successful enough to repeat the following week. When I forgot for the second time, there was no sympathy or saviours because now, I just looked like an obstructive pest, hell-bent on ruining the experience for everyone else. On this occasion, the teacher improvised, offering me a plain biscuit while everyone else had chocolate, and then it stopped, and the biscuit treat saga was no more.

So, this became my story of lack. Money made us different, and because of it, I was an outsider. Lack of money became intrinsically wired to the debilitating emotions of shame, but there was heavier baggage to carry. I'd told myself that I alone could solve my problems, and in trying to protect my mum's feelings, I'd taken on the responsibility of the parent.

When I reflect as an adult, I know my mum wouldn't have wanted me to suffer or feel left out. I know she'd have contacted the school or improvised with homemade cake. When it came to solving problems, Mum was an expert. Instead, I struggled silently, laying the foundations for a life full of responsibility, solving problems way above my capability. The beliefs we wire to shame can be the most debilitating of all, as they keep us locked in disconnection, isolated, or sitting on the outskirts of life, fearful of being seen. To move ourselves through this pattern, we have to send our compassion to that version of ourselves that dealt with the problem, acknowledging that we did our best at the time. We have compassion for that young girl who couldn't be truthful and carried the burden alone, and with an adult lens, we consider how the alternatives might have played out. What destructive beliefs might have been avoided or left unformed had an alternative path been taken?

When we have a desire to grow, these are the stories and beliefs we uncover along the way. They are painful but also freeing because we come to recognise our hidden coping strategies. They become so intrinsic to how we think and behave that they sit in our blind spot, becoming as solid as truth. Once we begin to bring them into the light, we get to examine them with the eyes of an adult and through this process, the beliefs that hold us back gradually lose their power and weaken their hold. Had the adults intervened, the young child might have learnt that people can be trusted and that adults have their back. This could have been a non-story where not having enough money isn't the end of the world, and the shame story never gets off the ground.

I've Got Nothing to Write About Guilt

I should have pointed out that this book follows the pathway of Hawkins' emotional scale, navigating through the most debilitating emotions to the most freeing with a little nod to my life history along the way. The emotional scale gives the book a structure, but with my obsessive hat on, does this mean I need a story for every emotion on his list?

Having conquered the battle of the shame stories, and believe me, that could possibly have been a book in its own right, the next stop on Hawkins' list is guilt. I have nothing! I have witnessed the pain of guilt, and this can be tough, particularly when we lose loved ones. Having observed its destructive nature in others, I've tried to sidestep it. I never like to leave situations on a sour note, so when I do experience guilt over my comments or behaviour, I address it by trying to make immediate amends.

I learnt this lesson painfully while supporting my elderly uncle. His favourite pastime seemed to be pushing my buttons, but he was also old and vulnerable. Whilst I wanted the satisfaction of defending myself against his cruel words, I came to realise that challenging someone with a heart condition wasn't going to make me feel better in the long run, especially if he decided to die on the spot just to teach me a lesson. I got better at taking a step back and moving the conversation in a more positive direction. I'm guessing there are people caring for difficult relatives who find themselves doing the same thing. It's more than keeping the peace or avoiding confrontation. It's recognising the higher stakes. Comments can be hurtful or even rile our anger, and it doesn't mean that this is acceptable behaviour. It's about recognising that it's not a battle worth fighting and reminding ourselves that we have limited time together. Taking him out for a drive was a great distraction and lifted both of our moods. So, there we have it. I didn't have a single thing to relate to on the topic of guilt.

I have not been in a rush to write my book; it's been more a case of thinking about a topic and allowing the appropriate words to flow out onto the page. I decided that I'd probably skip the guilt chapter altogether and shared this view with my husband one Saturday afternoon as I was pottering around the kitchen.

"After all," I said, "it's not like I have to cover every single emotion to make my point."

I was pleased with my decision. It meant I could move on with gusto, if anyone actually does that. Not only had I solved my missing chapter problem, but I'd have one less chapter to write and one less chapter to run through at least two refinements. Genius!

This had been a productive day. Three things off my to-do list!

What happened next was akin to Tom the cat being whacked in the face by Jerry's frying pan. For those of you who are too young for the reference, Tom and Jerry, the classic cat-and-mouse cartoon couple. To all the extremely busy women out there, constantly juggling, I send my apologies in advance for what you are about to read.

Less than twenty-four hours after ditching my guilt chapter, I was sitting in bed on Sunday morning, contemplating whether I felt ready to get up. I'd had breakfast in bed and two or three cups of tea. The time was edging its way towards lunchtime, very close, it was 12.01.

As I reflected on my easy morning in bed, I began to run through my week, totting up my hours of consultancy and coaching. How many hours had I spent on each? Had I done anything in the evenings that warranted work? Had I tweaked the website or done any planning? All of a sudden, here I was, trying to justify staying in bed on a Sunday morning. It hadn't even been a conscious decision; I'd just felt like taking it easy and switching off from the rest of the world. Isn't that what I tell people every single day? "Listen to your body. Try to break free from the mind."

For me, teaching has become an experience of great irony and a way of delivering truth to myself. How often have you been in the throes of giving advice when, even as the words are moving from the mind to the voice, you have that aha moment? The message of needing to hear those words yourself or heed the advice unveils itself with startling accuracy. If we choose to explore these messages, it's here that we have those moments of transformation. We all believe in our own powers of self-awareness, but it is possible to have blind spots that drive our behaviours or beliefs unchallenged. The startling resonance of these moments suggests that we need to delve a little deeper and bring something that has been lurking in the shadows into the light. It's a true turning point because once we become aware of this blind spot, we can never go back. The pattern may continue, but we will now observe it until it eventually loses its power. Mindfulness refers to these moments as insight. A point when we see our own patterns and observe them without judgement. When we are able to do this, the underlying cause often reveals itself.

So here I am on a Sunday morning, and it's now 12:10. As I recall my week and find myself trying to justify my rest instead of listening to my body, as the mind layers on the guilt, I suddenly realise that this is it, the missing chapter.

"I'd been looking for guilt in all of the wrong places!"

This was a sneaky, powerful guilt trip, and it wasn't just a Sunday special. I realised that I was continually totting up my hours, checking whether or not I'd worked hard enough to deserve that downtime. I'd had a successful week, but suddenly, the achievements and progress were a thing of the past, completely obliterated by guilt. A subtle message of not being good enough, not having worked hard enough and then the impending doom of some unforeseen punishment waiting for me. A failed business, a shitty book, all rewards for not quite making the grade and getting my bum out of bed on a Sunday morning.

The achievements of the week now become part of an accounting exercise, and there it is, deep within my psyche, measuring the hours worked and not the work delivered. This is the human struggle of simply being and tuning into what we need. We are driven by a quid pro quo mentality where all of our actions and consequences must balance. Rest is justified by hours worked, converting our life back to the hourly currency.

There's a parable about animals who are caged and are so conditioned that they do not leave the cage even when the doors are open. I've yearned to be measured by what I deliver rather than the hours worked, and here I am, running my own business, trapped in the old mindset. When I start work later than 9am, I'm programmed to finish late to ensure I've completed my full quota of hours.

Who is this tyrant who expects a forty-hour week with travel, whether it's productive or not?

Who is this tyrant who will allow me to write a chapter of my book in the morning and then search for productive ways to fill the afternoon hours?

Who is this tyrant who expects me to sit at my desk most of the day, knowing that I need to be outside getting fitter, healthier and more engaged with nature?

Who is this tyrant who keeps me trapped in my old ways when I'm constantly telling the rest of the world how to live more mindfully?

In *Atlas of the Heart,* Brown (2021) describes guilt as *'an emotion we experience when we fall short of our own expectations or standards'.*

This becomes apparent in the attempt to measure the working hours completed to justify the rest. When we're looking for the emotional patterns that keep us trapped in low energy or hijack our contentment, we expect them to be large, looming and on ceremony. I thought I knew guilt inside out, and yet there it was, hiding in the shadows. These are the small realisations that move us forward, and they become the nuggets of our awakening. Once they're revealed, we cannot unsee the power of their mental stories. We gradually come to truly know ourselves, and it's incremental. There's no grand finale where the Angel Gabriel descends in his Audi R8 and throws open the door, saying, "Jump in the car, kid, you're enlightened."

We take something out of the dark and bring it out into the light, and it cannot go back in. There's a conflict between how I want my life to be and how my mind insists on running it, and this is the work we all face. Today, I have stepped on a snake that's taken me back down the board. However, I only go back a few rows, no matter how it appears. Coming out of the other side of this programming is a challenge, but like everything in mindfulness, it's another move towards a more open and authentic version of me.

Apathy: Crying Into My Ice Cream

The city of Chester is absolutely beautiful. A collection of Tudor buildings line cobbled streets that weave their way down through the city walls towards the river. It's definitely a city for messing about on the river, particularly in springtime. It was the obvious choice for my 17th birthday party for three. We'd packed a picnic, bought a bottle of wine and headed down to hire a boat. The river was lined with beautiful cruisers offering onboard catering. They sail down the Dee at a leisurely pace, passing the deer in the grounds of Eaton Hall. Sadly, our budget didn't quite stretch that far, so we paid for an hour's rowing boat hire. Obviously, the birthday girl never rows and about ten minutes into our adventure, we decided that we'd gone far enough. It was now midday and late enough to open a bottle of wine. I wouldn't say that I'm a wine connoisseur despite my years of tasting, and at this age, having only experienced cheap wine with screw tops, we were a little bemused to be presented with a cork. As life emergencies go, this was pretty high up there, and I don't know whether it was the genetic resourcefulness of women or my Irish heritage that led us to the conclusion that we could push the cork in with the end of our umbrella. Fast forward twenty-three years, and on my fortieth birthday, I was able to hire a more grown-up boat and had ensnared more than three people into my friendship group. I have fond memories of the city, and if you know where to look, it's possible to find a riverside parking space. If you're exceptionally lucky, there'll be an ice cream van. This is where I had my 2003 meltdown, right here in the car park, ice cream in hand. I'd found myself in a predicament that I just couldn't solve, and I was torn up in this emotional turmoil. I didn't know how to move forward, but I knew I needed to get out of the office and find a quiet place to work through my thoughts. For some reason, water always seems to do the trick.

It had been coming for a few months. One morning in April, the role I thought couldn't get any worse took on an unexpected and equally dismal direction. I found myself working for a younger woman. In those days, I had no idea what triggers were, but I definitely had this one. Oh, how much I'd toiled endlessly to receive my promotion. Ambitious and highly motivated to achieve, my emotional vocabulary could not compute this new situation. It went against the order of things. I'd been well and truly pipped to the post. I had failed where she had succeeded.

Her appointment came as a result of her working closely with a small group of users to implement a system. When you work in technology, implementing systems is sort of the point of the role, and yet, for the last fifteen years, I've spent most of my time not implementing. Not me personally, but teams and teams of people, all working really hard but not getting across the finishing line. Set against the backdrop of a slow-paced organisation, her achievement was miraculous, and her appointment was duly deserved. However, I knew I'd also implemented systems many times over. The difference was that my experience had been gathered 'before', and it's a phenomenon that many of my peers have witnessed.

We sit in front of an interview panel and impress them with all of our experience. It lands us the role but seems to add no value when we seek out that ever-elusive promotion. Only experience that can be demonstrated within the current organisation seems to be considered. This contributed to my frustration, but through mutual respect, my new manager and I were able to get along very well, and I was even pacified with a small team of my own.

One of my responsibilities was to forecast the monthly work output of the team, a simple process where we assessed the work requests coming in from various departments and confirmed how much of that work the team could complete that month. The time spent was converted into chargeable days, which were invoiced to the appropriate departments. It was a simple process, but on this occasion, the work coming in didn't match the skill set of the team I was managing. Technical people work in languages much like the languages we share across countries. You cannot expect a developer who speaks Spanish to deliver something in French. I raised the issue with my new line manager, suggesting we factor in some downtime in our forecasts whilst we considered how to address the mismatch. For me, the problem was very clear and wasn't going to disappear without some sort of action. However, after escalating it to the senior management team, we were advised that as the demand of the overall department matched the delivery rate of the teams, there was nothing to worry about.

I spent the entire month scrabbling around for different courses or ad hoc projects to give to the team as they turned up at their desks daily with absolutely nothing to do. When it came to month-end, as predicted, the team hadn't contributed anything to the incoming demand. Now we had actual evidence, I was sure it would shift the leader's perspectives, particularly as the team were very demoralised. I was completely floored when my manager suggested that the downtime was okay, but the issue was that I hadn't forecast it in the first place. I was dumbfounded. It was as if the previous conversation hadn't happened, and there was no acknowledgement of the real problem. How would the situation ever improve? I knew I'd raised the issue, but no one had listened. I was so overwhelmed by a sense of betrayal and anger that I didn't have the emotional capacity to push back or challenge the statement without breaking down. The only option I had was to nod politely until I could escape and re-group. This is how I found myself staring at the river, surrounded by the birds and the trees, crying into my Mr Whippy.

I couldn't believe that I was this broken down over a job. Options, thoughts, and ideas were all spinning around in my head, but I had no idea how to solve the problem. It wasn't my line manager;

my concerns had been escalated right up the chain. No one was interested in the morale of my team or in taking responsibility. Their only response was to shift the blame. How could I exist in this culture of deceit, working with a team of people who had to turn up to work and pretend to be busy? It was soul-destroying, and I couldn't fix it. I didn't have a single answer, and I felt consumed by helplessness.

The only option I had was to remove myself from this environment. I literally couldn't bring myself to spend a moment longer than needed in this organisation.

When we remove ourselves from organisations, no one is interested in tales of ethics or morale. It can look like we are taking the moral high ground, an inferred slight on those people who stay. Yet I didn't leave to take a stand. I left because I didn't know how to stay. I didn't know how to work in an environment where people were paid to stare at their desks pretending to work. I couldn't be that person they looked to for answers when I was utterly powerless to do anything. I didn't know how to calmly push back against those people who could effect change because I was outraged by their behaviour. I didn't recognise that these problems I was trying to solve were not mine to carry. That world had stopped making sense to me, and the only way to navigate it was to completely shut down or to escape.

I was honest with those close to me, but our tribal instinct to save face meant that I needed a cover story. At the time, I was in a duo called Raw. We played acoustic music, and I'd recorded a couple of music CDs, so I told people I was giving up my career to be a full-time musician. It felt ridiculous and intangible, but it was easier to pitch this odd story than to say, I just cannot cope in this culture; it's diminishing my soul. Twenty years on, it seems more acceptable for people to take time out and review their life choices. It's seen as a courageous option, but I wasn't being brave; I was running away. As it turned out, there was a new adventure just around the corner.

Within a couple of weeks of handing in my notice, I was attending a charity event in Hoylake at a converted fire station. It was part of a crescent-shaped collection of buildings. I have no idea how I came to be walking around the other side of the crescent, but right there—ready to let—was an old locksmiths. I'd always dreamt of running a tea shop and could see from my workplace that the coffee culture was becoming popular. With beautiful, tall glass windows overlooking a picturesque church and close to the station, I knew this space would make the perfect coffee shop. Not just any coffee shop; this would be a coffee shop featuring arts and music. A place for my little duo to entertain and for other local up-and-coming musicians to play. The walls would be adorned with the work of local artists, giving the place a real community feel. This was my plan; it was located a few streets away from where I was born, so it was fate!

Whilst I was still employed, I applied for a bank loan for the renovation and also secured a bid from the Arts Council. Once I'd haggled with planning permission, the conversion began. It was expensive because not only had I paid rent during the planning stages, but one of the tenants in the flats above had complained about the change of use and the potential noise from musicians. Despite having lived above a locksmiths for decades, he insisted that the room be soundproofed, and this was one of the conditions of planning. It delayed the project and cost me thousands of pounds. Then, inconveniently, the tenant died the day before we opened—the nerve of him after I spent all of that money.

Cards on the table, I had absolutely no experience of running a coffee shop, but I had worked at McDonald's. Aside from the incident where I slipped on a gherkin and placed my hand on the quarter grill to stop myself from falling, it had gone quite well.

Although I guess, with hindsight, I was rude to the customer who asked for extra dips so he could stare down my top as I bent down to get them. I also woke up in the middle of the night shouting, "Do you want cheese on your quarter?" but aside from that, good, I think. I mean, how hard could it be?

Once planning was approved, we got started on the demolition of the inner fixtures and fittings. Having brothers who love to destroy things, often not on purpose, has its bonuses. After a few hours of enduring their *Chuckle Brothers* impressions, providing them with bacon butties, cakes and drinks, the site was cleared.

I wanted the shop to have an authentic French pavement café feel and chose slate tiles for the floor, as well as a rich wine colour for the feature walls. I dug out all of my old sheet music from the loft and used it to decorate some of the walls, varnishing it to make it look aged. It was such an exciting project, and I spent hours on eBay searching for the right furniture. I got completely carried away and, much to the annoyance of my husband, sourced the fittings from all over the country. Had I been a bit savvier, there were cheaper and less time-consuming ways to fit out the store, but here I was, running my own business, shaping my future and loving every single minute of it.

I was absolutely beside myself when I 'won' tables and chairs to support fifty covers, a wooden counter and a large patisserie fridge. My plan was to collect the fifty covers, furnish the shop with half of them and then sell the rest. Like the great game of Britain, we hired a van and travelled to the end of the country to collect them. However, there was one small snag, and I have the perfect excuse. When I was a child, I didn't have one of those blue plastic balls with cut-out shapes. They were designed to help children match the correct shape with the correct hole and then push the object through. This is how we ended up with a van that couldn't accommodate fifteen tables, fifty chairs, a patisserie fridge and a sales counter. We collected the overpriced patisserie fridge, filled the rest of the van up with chairs and tables then gave our apologies for leaving the rest behind. I had to resell the counter and get the new buyer to collect it. They messed the vendor around, and all in all, everyone else became a little bit agitated. I was still energised by the excitement of my new coffee shop and did not have time for agitation.

I completed my French theme with chandelier lights. This required a slight upgrade to the fuse box. After planning delays and the refurbishment, the coffee shop was finally up and running. The musicians were booked in, and the walls were adorned with the work of local artists.

The chandeliers would become the bane of my life because when some of the musicians plugged their kit in, they'd blow the entire fuse box. Some argued that it only blew up if their playing coincided with putting the kettle on, and I do remember sitting in the dark whilst one of the customers asked me if he was likely to get his cup of tea.

When it came to market research, I did this as I went along, using graphs and spreadsheets to work out the best hours to open. This is how I came to be open seven days a week, 9:00 - 5:30. I had part-time help, but I tried to schedule this around the footfall, and it was completely unpredictable. The shop could be empty for hours, and then multiple tables would turn up at once. The first bank holiday weekend was so busy that we ran out of food and crockery within a few hours, and the place was chaos. The following week, there were four staff standing around doing nothing. There simply was no pattern. Worst of all, after paying the staff, I wasn't even earning minimum wage. After going from the refurbishment to opening, I clocked forty-two days of continuous work in the shop.

I was so physically and mentally exhausted that on day forty-two, I locked the door and sat on the loo, crying my eyes out.

I thought that being my own boss would solve all of my problems, but having escaped one type of stress, I'd created a stressful environment all of my own. I had changed my external world, but the inner world was still the same. I was still driven by the same beliefs and behaviours, thinking I had to do everything alone. The title of Jon Kabat-Zinn's book sums it all up: *Wherever You Go, There You Are!*

Grief: Finding Your Path and Your Pace

I've heard that grief is a process, but I've never found this analogy useful. It suggests that we move seamlessly from one phase to another until, eventually, we're all right again and can return to normal. It diminishes an experience that leaves us feeling completely debilitated and maybe even questioning the entire point of carrying on with life. This is the severe depression I found myself drowning in at the age of twenty-four.

After the end of yet another toxic relationship, one that my mum had warned me about, I found myself living at home. In some ways, it felt good to be back on the old estate, albeit in a different flat. We'd lived there for around twelve years as I grew up, and just a year after I started college in Yorkshire, Mum had moved with her new partner to a different estate so that she could have a house with a garden. After three years, she'd moved back to the same block but was now on the ground floor. There wasn't a private garden, but it wasn't long before Mum adopted the communal garden. She planted sweet peas and carnations, bringing much-needed colour to the space. Historically, I'd been bullied because we lived in a council flat, but that aside, it was a lovely place to live. We were surrounded by trees and fields, both front and back. There were acres of woods to explore, hidden ponds and a nearby dairy farm with cows and horses. We made dens in ditches and even had access to a perfectly formed bamboo circle, which we called the 'caneeys'. When I started college in Yorkshire and travelled back early on a Monday morning, I loved cutting through the woods, completely engulfed by the sound of early morning birdsong and the gentle rustling of the leaves on the trees. Returning home after yet another failed relationship felt like going backwards, but I had a lot to be thankful for. Mum was always a constant staple in my life. At a deep level, I knew she always had my back, even when she was challenging my decisions or beliefs.

It was an ordinary Sunday; Mum's partner, Reg, had gone off to stay with his mum, and I'd recently given up my Sunday night shift at the local pub, so Mum and I were home alone. It was the simple pleasures that brought Mum joy, and she particularly liked the fact that I had a car. We'd been shopping at B & Q in the morning, and that evening, she was in the mood for a few episodes of *Prisoner Cell Block H*, a good film and some fries, "Like those they have in America," she said. This was the 1990s when the nearest McDonald's was five miles away and most shops were closed on Sundays. So, we drove about a mile and a half to a little mini-market in search of frozen French fries and then settled down for the evening. That's my recollection of the last day we spent together. I was woken in the night by Mum coughing and often wondered whether I should have paid more attention, but Mum had a constant smoker's cough, so it wasn't unusual. The song of the blackbird was in full flow the next morning as I made my way out to the car. I was driving to Chester to meet my boss before driving down to a customer's site in Oxford.

I was partway through a client meeting when someone entered the room and passed me a note to ring the office. Had I paid more attention, I'd have seen that they'd circled the word urgent. I didn't, so it would be an hour before I called the office. They told me to call a hospital nurse. The lady on the phone had a kind voice but couldn't give me any details. She urged me to return home as soon as possible. So began the longest drive ever from Oxford to Chester and then Chester to the hospital. I often wonder why we didn't drive straight to the hospital and collect the car the next day. It's a cruel trick of the mind when we imagine that the facts we have after the event were available to us at the time. Had we known better, we'd have done things differently. We can't apply those facts retrospectively. Hindsight can be painful.

It was October, and it was dark by the time I reached the hospital on that Monday evening. I went to the desk to track down the ward and then made my way to the lifts. Arriving at the lift doors, I bumped into my stepmother, Linda, also on her way to the ward. I was so relieved to see her and to find out what was going on. As I spoke, the lift arrived and we entered it with a group of people. Linda was eerily quiet. I was getting a sense that things were wrong. As we arrived at the correct floor, I turned to her again as we stepped out into the open corridor.

"Is it really serious?" I said.

"I'm sorry," she said. "Your mum died about an hour ago."

We shuffled into the ward, where most of my family occupied the waiting room. Distant relatives I hardly knew were eating sandwiches like they were on some sort of family day out. My dad walked over to me, closely followed by a nurse. It was too soon to receive messages of condolences. I didn't want confirmation. I braced myself for her compassionate comment and was shocked when she stressed the urgency of me seeing Mum quickly, as having her on the ward was distressing the other patients. How could she expect me to consider the distress of others, of strangers, five minutes after hearing my own mum was gone forever? I resented her lack of compassion but moved forward as my dad led me up to the room where Mum was lying—a long corridor, just one step in front of the other, walking to hell. I wanted to climb on the bed and cling to her forever, but I couldn't move. I had so much to say, but I couldn't fit a lifetime into that moment. After what seemed so little time to say goodbye, I was ferried back to the waiting room. After some milling around, we all went home because what else was there to do?

I remember the pain across my forehead from hours of sobbing, experiencing the sort of grief that almost convulsed my body. It erupted from a well so deep within that I wondered if it would ever stop. It did, temporarily, when I'd worn myself out, but there was no escape in sleep, just hours of lying awake thinking and feeling that unbearable pain. For weeks, I was trapped in my mind, continually asking, "Why did you leave me?" "What did I do wrong?" I often visualised a lone baby bear trapped on a mountaintop, surrounded by wilderness. Ironically, a few weeks later, I did move into a top-floor flat. My only comfort was that Mum had viewed it with me a few months earlier.

The mornings were the hardest. I'd often have nightmares that Mum was seriously ill, and I was trying to save her. I'd wake up searching for some relief from this torment, only to find that the situation was even worse. Some mornings, I'd lie in bed thinking about the years of life stretching out before me, empty. When I drove my car to work, there was a particular bend that required me to slow down, and I wondered if keeping my foot on the pedal would make the pain go away.

What finally got me moving forward was drugs, a specialised bereavement counsellor and music. My mum loved the messages in music and was a big Dolly Parton fan, so when Whitney Houston released Dolly Parton's 'I Will Always Love You' a few weeks later, it felt like a direct message from Mum. October 1993 was a dreadful time, but this time I found comfort in Mariah Carey's 'Hero'. When I heard the lyrics 'strength to carry on', I knew somewhere buried deep within was an inner strength I had to call on.

My life became functional, but it would take twenty years for the anger to shift, and I remember feeling it lift. It was on Mum's anniversary, and I was walking up from the Pier Head to Liverpool Cathedral to light a candle. I suddenly became aware that I wasn't angry anymore, and it felt like I'd released a huge weight. I greeted this palpable shift with my usual gallows humour. Laughing to myself, I said, "Wow, that took a while." On reflection, I realised I'd been struggling with acceptance. The word highlights the importance of language and what we infer from it because, somewhere in my interpretation, acceptance meant okay. I can never accept that this life-changing event was okay, but I can come to terms with the acknowledgement because it is a recognition of truth. It's an invitation to let go of the all-consuming power of denial and resistance. These emotions can keep us very stuck, but we can begin to loosen their grip.

When I lead retreats, I'm very cautious about what I share, aware that people often attend to get some much-deserved peace of mind. The May 2024 retreat was popular, and for some reason, grief became a prominent theme for the group, with many attending to get respite from the painful thoughts that were plaguing them. On this occasion, I discussed my experience. I talked about the anger I'd held on to for so long and how the turning point for me was acknowledgement rather than acceptance. I chose my words carefully because it's delicate, and sometimes what we express as empathy appears to redirect the attention away from someone's grief and back onto our own. The timing of the subject was odd, particularly as at the end of the same month, I found myself dealing with my own grief when my uncle passed away suddenly. Like any death, it seems disingenuous to describe the passing as sudden because his health had been deteriorating for some time, but he'd developed a sort of bounce-back resilience that had me believing he'd be around forever.

I was on the last day of a trip to Italy when the police phoned to deliver the news. Despite his age and ill health, when the day finally came, it was shocking and painful. It was excruciating navigating the trip home and being out on show when my overwhelming desire was to curl into a ball and sob. I wasn't prepared for grief. I only expected to feel relief. My uncle had been struggling with his health and confidence since the passing of his wife five years earlier. She'd had dementia, and he had looked after her. For many years, our relationships had been solely focused on how they survived these challenges of old age. It was difficult and tiring. I'd decided I was beyond grief, like the emotional choice was mine.

I had grieved along the way. Small pockets of it threatened to engulf me when I looked at what they had become. I grieved for her, and my heart broke for him, watching his one true love fade away. Then it was his turn to fade. With his sallow cheeks and seven-stone frame, I worried that he was starving himself to death. The emotional pain was inconvenient. It wouldn't have allowed me to carry on with all of those practical things that just needed to be done. So, I stopped looking too closely and just did what I could because we cannot support those whom we care for when we're falling apart ourselves. When he finally passed away, the arguments and the stress that seemed to define our relationship in the final years faded away. They became irrelevant, and all I could see in the photographs was the fun side of his personality. It was almost as though I missed the very soul of him and everything else had just been fog.

The entire ritual of death is emotionally exhausting, and we're forced to share this difficult, personal experience with complete strangers as we navigate our way through official processes. We unintentionally find ourselves on a conveyor belt, completing the necessary tasks, but it gives us a focal point. Strangely, there is meaning in arranging the ceremony, our last act of giving for the one we have lost. Once the big day is over and there are no more plans, there is space in the mind for strange thoughts and questions. *Where are they? Why did they leave me?* With every odd question that arises, there's an alternative part of the mind that knows the answer and also knows that the questions are irrational. It's the oddest experience ever. A constant battle with a reality that half of our mind resists.

There's no doubt that our thoughts contribute to the all-consuming emotional pain. This is not a time to use logic or attempt to quantify our feelings by comparing them with others. When we do, we're at risk of diminishing this very personal experience. Is it harder to live with the pain of missing someone who has been a part of our lives for over sixty years? Do we have the capacity to take comfort from a life well-lived when we are consumed by grief? Should we grieve more for the child whose life is cut short, grieving for the loss of their soul as well as the opportunities they'll never experience? Grief for the life we knew and the life they will never know.

When someone dies after a long illness, we can grieve each time we notice them fading away and again when they finally pass. As a carer, the loss might be accompanied by exhaustion as we often push through, finding the strength to support them. The well-intentioned advice we receive often has an underlying message that we should eventually return to normal. Those polite words of comfort carry a subtle nudging and chivvying, re-directing us back to the path of normality. Yet the normality we once knew has gone forever and clinging to the idea of its return can keep us stuck in one place. Only when we're ready can we gradually begin to carve a new path as, little by little, we move towards a different way of being. It's not for others to direct us because grief is an individual journey. Eventually, we learn to live alongside this pain until its ache fades into something that doesn't consume our every moment.

Hawkins (2013) places the emotional energy of grief right between apathy and fear. Yet, for me, it's a cocktail of emotions ranging from the dullness of apathy to the fiery power of anger. It bounces between apathy, depression, guilt and anger, sometimes all at once, so describing it as a process can diminish its complexity. Perhaps it's the necessary yin and yang of these opposing energies that give us the power to lift ourselves from what feels like the depths of despair. Sometimes it seems like we will never feel any different, but there isn't a timetable for grief. It is often the expectations we place on ourselves that lead to frustration and a desire to banish emotions that aren't quite ready to move on. Journalling can help to free up our cyclic thoughts. It's a gentle approach which requires us to let our thoughts flow uninhibited onto the page. Seeing our ideas on the page can provide insight into where we are getting stuck, even enough to help us inch through a particularly difficult spell because that's what life is: a series of emotional episodes.

As we observe the flow of our emotions and come to terms with their impermanent nature, there is hope that over time, the heavier emotions will lift a little or appear less often, giving us space to experience more humour, love or joy. In the words of Rumi (circa 1250), we must experience it all, and the movement of emotions gives us hope of lighter days ahead. Observing and honouring our emotions, just as they are, holds the power to move forward, safe in the knowledge that even grief, as heavy and as awful as it is, it will pass. We cannot hurry or cajole it. We must sense what feels right for us, finding our own path at our own pace.

Fifty Shades of Fear: The Fat Chapter!

It's very unprofessional to have a fat chapter, but when it comes to fear, I feel I have a lot to say. It's probably where my journey started, although I say that with the benefit of hindsight. At the time, I didn't know I was on this journey; I didn't have a plan, and I definitely wouldn't describe myself as fearful. That's the great mystery of the language we speak every day. We all know fear and have witnessed it or experienced it. My brother tells me he is not scared of flying but of crashing, and it seems rational that something that potentially threatens our very existence elicits fear. Mentally digesting all of the safety statistics in the world will not get my brother onto that plane. Yet the perceived experience of joy and some strong beer in the airport lounge is enough to motivate him to go through the pain of sparking up his nervous system for a few hours. So, here is a fear we see and understand. We can file it under rational.

Unless you live in Australia, where spiders are large and deadly, the fear of these eight-legged ninjas seems less rational. Even as I write, I can physically cringe at the thought of those spindly little legs running towards me. Seeing particularly large spiders on TV is enough to make my back arch like my cat does when he's spooked and does his funny little monkey walk. You might even be wincing as you read. Yet the funny thing about this fear is that it was something I learnt. I remember the scene when my mum saw a large spider on the living room ceiling and screamed. At the time, my uncle shouted at her, saying she would teach me to be scared. I remember thinking the idea was ridiculous as I wasn't scared at all, but I so wanted to be like Mum and impress her. I wanted her to think we were the same, so I pretended to be scared. Unfortunately, I can't remember when pretending turned into real fear and twenty years on, I found myself frozen to the spot with my legs shaking as I tried to place a glass over a large spider in the hallway. I couldn't get close enough for fear that it would start running. Until recently, I'd filed this memory away, and once I realised it was taught, I became curious about whether I could unpick it. As I try to become more connected to a natural world comprising many species, the sense that these creatures are here to harm me seems more ludicrous, and I am trying to let them be.

The fears we can see are easier to work with, but fear is a lurker; it has many faces, some of which are not instantly recognisable as fear. Our society has multiple labels for it, but one industry that has a real handle on it is the media. As we innocently settle in to watch that fascinating documentary about the life of the Arctic penguin, we're reeled into the life of Percy the penguin. We see his parents struggling to guard his egg, watching his birth and buying into his backstory, observing the powers of nature with awe and contentment. Just as we're settling into our fairytale, the voice of the presenter becomes edgy, the music changes and within a few seconds, the mood shifts as we're reminded that Percy the penguin might not make it to next year because we used an aerosol deodorant in 1988.

When we momentarily leave Percy's plight, the charity adverts continually remind us not to get too complacent because we're surrounded by hardship, and whilst one in four people used to be at risk from cancer, it's now one in two. It's not safe to be happy people.

I'm not against sharing, and it's our natural instinct to want to help, but the emotional demands on our minds and bodies far outweigh our capacity to deal with them. The consumer is often held responsible for issues beyond their control, which can leave us feeling guilty, helpless and just a little bit on edge. Edginess isn't just a sensation but an indication that our nervous system is heightened, and we have stress hormones pumping through our bodies. We're so caught up with the stuff that goes on in our heads that we have little awareness of living in low states of anxiety. Even if we notice, these sensations can feel very normal. This is true of my experience when I realised that I worried a lot. In my first professional role as an IT consultant, I thought the feelings that I'd now label as anxiety were normal. On my first solo trip down south, driving to London for the first time, feeling nervous on the journey seemed perfectly rational. What wasn't was an overactive sense of messing up. I envisaged myself driving around London, not knowing where I was going and getting in everyone's way. I would be the one holding everyone up because I didn't know what I was doing. This impossible belief system sees everyone else as being completely on top of their game, whilst I'm floundering around just getting in everyone's way. This was my interpretation of how everyone in the world saw me—yes, even those millions of people I'd never met. The fear that the world and the people in it are hostile is one of the most separating fears we have. It makes us wary of meeting new people, who pick up on our distance and perceive us as aloof when we're actually working out whether we feel safe in their company. It's a sense that we're not good enough in a way that makes us eager to please, not for the sake of pleasing itself but because our very survival depends on it. I've come to liken it to the M6 toll road. If you've only ever travelled down the M6, then your mindset will be one of planning for the traffic, minimising its impact and then judging yourself when you end up in the inevitable queue around junction 10. There are people who have only ever travelled down the M6 toll road and, without experiencing the pain of congestion, have a completely different outlook on life, expecting the road to be easy and coping well with adversity should it arise. The real transformation starts when we recognise that maybe our mindset has been shaped and programmed through childhood experiences and whilst we cannot go back and change them, we do have an opportunity to travel down a different route, one that begins to unpick everything that went before. We can get onto the M6 toll road and experience more ease, realising that there is a different way of being in life.

It took me a long time to reach this particular conclusion because I lacked emotional literacy. The first indication I had that something wasn't quite right occurred when I began referring to myself as stressed. When my friend and I went off for our annual spa break, and once again I found myself asking the therapist for a calming treatment, I began wondering if things would ever be any different.

I'd started my career in a small company that I'd describe as a little bit chaotic. At twenty-two years old, I was confident enough to believe that there was nothing I couldn't solve with ability and hard work. It was easy to stand out, and my work was recognised and rewarded. This motivated me to take on more responsibility and work even harder, but at some point, something changed. What was once interpreted as me going above and beyond became the expectation. I began to feel that I needed to give 110% every day just to keep on top of my work. Some of the responsibilities I took on lay beyond my own capability, so I was often dependent on the managing director, who was the technical subject matter expert. My commitment to resolving issues for the customer wasn't always supported by practical help as the technical expert had other priorities. The frustration of letting people down and the perceived lack of support tipped my attitude over into resentment. Now struggling just to get through the day, it wasn't long before I had to take time off with stress. Over the course of my career, I moved to a larger company where other people held the same role. The pace of work was slower, and I worked as part of a team, sharing the same experience of what was a difficult and problematic project. I could see so many ways to solve the issues, and I absolutely thrived. I saw this as a great opportunity to prove what I could do and to get the promotion to the next grade. When I started, my line manager was very supportive, and we had an excellent relationship. However, he left and was replaced by someone who just didn't seem up to the role. I'd known this manager before; we'd worked on a charity event together. I'd warmed to him and we got on well, but now that he was my manager, I was literally drowning in his ineptitude. He had the title, the role and the grade that I aspired to, and yet there wasn't a single thing about his ability that inspired me. Whilst I was on site at 5am nervously supporting the system implementations and suffering from a sleepless night, he joked about sitting at home relaxing in his PJs, munching on his Shreddies. Professional on the outside but seething on the inside, I amused myself by wondering if it was possible for someone to drown face down in a tablespoon of milk and a gathering of mushy Shreddies. Whilst I found the experience taxing, I had gotten into a rhythm of working with the senior leaders to agree on the priorities and workload for the team. It was always a challenge as they always wanted more work than we could physically deliver, but as we consistently met their deadlines, they came to trust my opinion. It was all going so well until my manager decided to do his actual job. I don't know whether it was an attempt by the senior management team to force him to pull his weight, but that's when it all went wrong. The next thing I knew, he'd gone off agreeing our workload with the senior leadership team. I absolutely dreaded the outcome. True to form, he returned with a set of demands that was double the capacity of the team.

When I challenged it, he told me to get on with it and not knowing what else to do, I escalated the problem to his manager. I was shocked when this led to me being removed from the team. All of those endless hours fielding issues, managing the workload and working with a lovely team of people, gone overnight.

I'd thrown everything I had into it. Losing the project that had completely consumed me for eighteen months left me feeling empty and directionless. I took some reassurance when my role was filled by three people, as it really brought home to me how much I'd been doing. Once I no longer had the distraction or momentum of this all-consuming focus, I fell ill with complete physical and mental exhaustion. I felt completely broken to the core and was diagnosed with work-related stress and depression.

One of the questions I asked myself again and again was why I couldn't cope. *How did other people just take this in their stride? What was wrong with me?*

The Stress Epidemic: Is it Just Me?

I thought it was just me who found the corporate world a little taxing and confusing. I thought it was just me who had a work persona that said, "I'll do that, leave it with me," on the outside, but on the inside was crying, "Why me?"

That sense of brokenness began to slowly untangle when I started studying mindfulness. As my story unfolded, it became clear that constant worrying was only part of the picture. With hindsight, I had anxiety bubbling away. It wasn't something I'd even considered until I was called out by another student on my course.

As part of our final year dissertation, we were asked to outline our proposals for research, and I identified stress as my topic of study. The students gathered as a group to share ideas, challenge assumptions and generally support each other. When I talked through my proposal, I was absolutely taken aback when one of the other students asked, "How are you perceiving stress?" *Well, it's just obvious, isn't it?* I thought to myself as I seethed silently, feeling very defensive over the entire thing. It's usually these little blows to our ego that give us some insight into our gremlins.

One of my triggers is not being the smartest person in the room, so I can struggle with being challenged, even when I know the intention is positive. It's not an arrogance thing. It's a deep wound that I uncovered during my insight practice, which I will explain later on. For now, it's important to recognise that sometimes our triggers can spur us on to find out more. Whether we like it or not, the fear of not knowing or not succeeding can ignite our motivation, whilst others are motivated by the anticipation of reward. Neither approach is right or wrong, but knowing which category we fall into can help us to use our natural tendencies to our advantage.

Spurred on by my imaginary academic thrashing, I vowed to leave no stone unturned in finding out what stress actually is. I hammered away on my keyboard, expecting to have the topic boxed off that morning. How hard could it be to Google a few definitions? I wanted a few sentences to describe stress and then a few words that explained the difference between stress and anxiety, because they were starting to look quite similar to me. This would be how I'd open my dissertation. Yet, the harder I dug, the more complicated it became. There were numerous health websites that listed the conditions, but no clear definition was provided.

Furthermore, oh, I do love a 'furthermore', there seemed to be a great overlap between the symptoms listed for stress and those listed for anxiety. When I explained this struggle to my lecturer, she advised me to go back to 1956 when Hans Selye helped to define stress in a physiological context. Selye specialised in stress research. He didn't have complex equipment, so his experiments were basic, but he was able to create a repeatable response in rats placed under duress.

When subjected to a set of particular conditions, they initially became stronger, but their health began to decline when they were continuously exposed, eventually demonstrating subdued behaviour and developing ulcers on the lining of their stomachs.

Selye brought the term 'stress' into being within this context. Whilst he initially experimented with the physiological stress response, his work was beginning to extend to the anticipatory aspect of stress. He discovered that rats could be primed to show the signs of stress through perceived rather than actual threats. This finding has been upheld by MRI research that is unpacking the impact that worrisome thoughts can have on our stress reaction. Selye's initial definition of stress related to the rat's response, and in human terms, it translates to *'a physiological, emotional and cognitive response to some form of trigger that takes us beyond what we can reasonably deal with.'*

Unfortunately, his definition was lost in translation and was used to describe both the reactions of the rats and the environmental conditions that caused that reaction. For example, in today's world, we might refer to a stressful environment. For clarity, the inner reaction of the stress response system is aligned with Selye's definition of stress. In contrast, the factors that contribute to the reaction are known as triggers or stressors. It's useful to make this distinction as tackling stress requires one approach for dealing with our stress response and a different one for managing the external triggers. With Selye's research underway as early as the 1950s, you may be wondering why we aren't further ahead in our understanding of this state. Some literature suggests there was an uprising of interest in psychoanalysis, popularised by Freud's revelations about our dreams, hidden thoughts and strange relationships with our parents. Whilst the timelines are difficult to map, this diversion narrowed focus on understanding the mind and came at the expense of appreciating the connections between our physiological and psychological reactions. To add more complexity, there's a third dimension to our experience that was definitely marginalised as evidenced in the fascinating book, *The Emotional Life of Your Brain*. Authors Davidson & Begley (2012) were advised by the scientific community that researching emotions was equivalent to career suicide. Ironically, it was through studying emotions that I made a breakthrough in my mission to define the difference between stress and anxiety. I was curious about why stress or anxiety didn't appear on the Hawkins (2013) emotional map, and yet the answer was simple. They are both related to 'fear', the strongest and fastest survival instinct in the body.

The fear response system is a physiological reaction that mobilises the major systems in the body and is initiated through the oldest part of our brain, the thalamus. With its connections to both the nervous system and the brain's alarm system, this grey matter can monitor our perception of threat and set off a chain reaction. The brain doesn't take any chances. While the amygdala searches the hippocampus for memories that identify the threat, the hypothalamus pituitary axis manages the sympathetic nervous system and the release of hormones into the bloodstream.

The hormone adrenaline prepares us for physical readiness, speeding up our heart rate to increase the flow of blood to major organs. We can experience a tight stomach, palpitations and tunnelled vision as the body prepares us to stave off the imminent threat. The body simultaneously slows down non-essential functions such as the immune and digestion systems.

Whilst we are reacting to our threat, the body works hard to return us to a state of balance, referred to as homeostasis. Selye (1956) concluded that mobilising the stress response in conjunction with the efforts to return to homeostasis is an extreme state of hyperarousal, and the body's continued efforts to adapt eventually led to exhaustion.

In human beings, it's the role of our executive function to assess our experience and determine whether the threat is real. The executive function is a collection of neural pathways that we form in childhood. They behave like muscles, meaning each time we follow a particular route, it becomes stronger and more powerful. If we experienced an over-controlling parent and our reaction was frustration or anger, each time our brain sees a similar situation, we respond in the same way. This might be inappropriate, but each time we react in this way, we strengthen that neural pathway so the executive part of the brain doesn't downgrade the threat. Our automatic reaction validates the threat and upholds it. If our childhood reaction to being controlled was to shut down or withdraw, we'll find ourselves closing down emotionally until we can physically retreat to safety.

The challenge with managing our stress response is that sometimes the trigger is internal. When Davidson & Begley (2012) used MRI scanning to analyse the impact of meditation on the brain matter, they made an interesting discovery. They asked a group of subjects to raise their right hand so they could observe which part of the brain lit up on the MRI scanner. The same group was then asked to think about raising their right hand but to keep completely still. The scientists discovered that the same region of the brain lit up even though the students hadn't moved. Further studies led them to conclude that the brain responds to thoughts about a threat in the same way it does to an actual threat.

If we find ourselves working with a difficult colleague and this leads us to feel anxious or irritated, mulling over the events or anticipating new encounters will re-ignite or prolong our exposure to those stressful feelings. The mind has the power to prevent the stress response system from resetting to its desired state of homeostasis. The same research team also identified a part of the brain that is on the lookout for threats when the mind is at rest. The default mode network lies in wait and can trigger random thoughts. Choden & Regan-Addis (2017), authors of the *Mindful*

Living Course book, suggest that these thoughts enter the mind without invitation, already laden with their powerful emotions.

Being human is complex and our vulnerability to stress is impacted by a number of factors, which can be genetic, historic, current and all of the above. All too easily, we get trapped in the content of the stories that surround stress, and there are multiple variations of life experiences and conditions that can have a bearing on how we feel. We look for answers to validate our experience, fearing we'll be judged. We care whether we are labelled as stressed or anxious. We care about the perception of the term 'mental health'. We fear anything that puts us at risk of banishment from our tribe. This can stop us moving forward. Yet what's absolutely clear is that we all have the equipment to become stressed or anxious.

How we use language matters. Whilst I was happy with the kudos of having work-related stress, I wasn't so sure about anxiety. The former suggests responsibility or overworking; the latter is often linked to a disorder. The labels imply professional kudos versus an implied weakness, and yet the body doesn't know the difference. Titles and labels matter. I've acquired a few in my time, my ultimate favourite being 'Scrum Master'. Ever since I came across this term, I wanted a piece of the action. I wasn't that fussed on the skills, but I definitely loved the title. I imagined the crowd gathering with anticipation. I'd stride into the office, cloaked in my long black coat like Keanu Reeves in *The Matrix*. "Make way, I am a Scrum Master," throwing my bendy keyboard onto the desk like a true technical professional. This was my moment. I'd worked in IT for over twenty-five years. Finally, it was becoming cool to be nerdy. I had not been this smug since Kim Kardashian made big bums fashionable. During my 'Scrum Master' indoctrination, the course facilitator referred to one of the activities as 'backlog refinement'. She also mentioned that it used to be called backlog grooming but the British have broken the term 'grooming'.

It made me wonder if we've also broken the term 'mental health' and whether, like Hebb's (1949) wiring analogy, it's only ever been linked to negative mental health. When I was growing up, mental health was synonymous with being sectioned in institutions such as Bedlam. We even called the fool or clown of the group 'mental', using it as a derogatory term. There's never been an interpretation of mental health that intuitively embraced a well mind. Whilst the term continues to be associated with illness, it taps into the tribal nature of our being. Our genetic survival depends on being a strong part of our group, and discussing mental health issues can compromise our existential safety. This is what the mind is trying to overcome when we have an open conversation.

As I learnt more about the complexities of the fear response and the delicate nature of our neural pathways, I became curious about why more people are not impacted by stress-related illnesses. Unfortunately, when I opened Pandora's Box, it became clear that stress is an epidemic costing companies in the region of £35 billion per year, Centre for Mental Health (2018). In 2019, 12.8 million working days were lost to stress, depression and anxiety, Health and Safety Executive (2019).

These figures only include the working population, 55% of which said they'd lie about a mental illness to protect their careers, Slater & Gordon (2014).

Whilst our mind can prevent us from resetting the stress response, the cortisol hormone can stay in the body for up to two hours, meaning that if we're triggered within this period, we are literally just topping up our hormones. Our awareness of feeling stressed can also contribute, particularly if we begin to detect that we are struggling to control our anger or fearful of breaking down in tears. These additional fears now co-exist alongside the original one.

Prolonged exposure leads to exhaustion. According to Maté (2003), modern illnesses such as autoimmune disease and fibromyalgia could be linked to an overactive fear response. Maté (2003) further suggests links to Alzheimer's and some cancers. Our mental and emotional health fluctuates along a continuum that can easily tip from wellness to poor health. There are adverse experiences that can make some of us more prone to challenges; however, most of us continually navigate maintaining this subtle balance. As human beings, we are uncomfortable with uncertainty, and the fear of the unknown can make us prone to controlling every aspect of our external world. This isn't a feasible use of our energy. But when external factors leave us feeling on edge, it can be beneficial to understand how our mind contributes to the story. This prevents the stress system from standing down. Our true gift is catching fear in the moment, identifying it as it arises. As we become aware of our fears, we can learn to intercept the cycle of those thoughts that ramp up our response. We can re-channel our energy, and one of the most powerful energies we have is anger.

Would You Like Sauce with That?

Anger isn't something we like to talk about in polite circles, unless, of course, it's happening to someone else. We describe people as having anger management problems, as if that particular dark energy had never tapped on our door. Yet there's a real energetic power in anger. When we grieve and we feel apathy, the weight of the world rests on our shoulders, and we might wonder what the point is. When anger enters the equation, we're empowered to act. It propels us in some way. That temper tantrum is anger leaving the body, but it's not British to be angry. We express our emotions through tutting or a loud, emphatic tut if things get really serious. Pema Chodron is a Tibetan Buddhist and author. In her writings on compassion, she explains that when we suppress anger, it goes down to the basement and lifts weights. I've heard counsellors refer to unexpressed anger as a bubbling volcano. Author of *Emotional Alchemy*, Bennett-Goleman (2002) suggests that people who love confrontation and always want to cause a row, are wracked with anger. Their desire to release it causes them to create situations that warrants their outbursts.

In my early twenties, I lived with a man who had a soul full of anger. Like most toxic relationships, we rarely see it coming because during the first few months, we're in some sort of honeymoon period where everyone is on their best behaviour. By day, he was an easy-going, go-lucky sort of person with a great sense of humour. By night, an abusive bully who looked for a row. He'd wait until we were out with friends and then make cruel comments to upset me. It was always done surreptitiously, so I'd be the one sitting at the table crying and looking unhinged. Initially, there would always be a reason why it was my fault. The last time it was my fault; we'd argued about the shortest route home. I could sense the rising tide of his anger, and when we got back to the house, I went upstairs out of his way. It wasn't long before he followed me up with a carton of chips in his hand. There was nothing he couldn't feel annoyed about, and, on this occasion, it was the fact that I'd escaped upstairs out of his way. He told me he'd put extra ketchup on his chips just for the joy of throwing them at my head. Then he did. This was the last of many straws; we split up, and I went back home to Mum. Between her passing away and me buying a flat, we seemed to drift back together.

I should have known better. My mum had warned me that she recognised his type and she was right. My new flat was about five miles from the old family home and from the local pub where I'd worked when I first met him. He had his weekends mapped out between the betting shop, the pub and Sunday lunch at his mum's. It wasn't that obvious to me because I worked in his local pub and saw him all weekend. When I emigrated to the next village, it became clear that the only way we were going to see each other was in that pub. During our early days, we'd driven out to Wales and had a picnic together. I wonder if this gave me some sort of false hope. It only happened the once because his friends started to call him Mr Picnic. For some reason, he found this disturbingly offensive.

We'd been to other places too, but on reflection, they were always nights out with his mates and their girlfriends. My insubordinate move away from his local pub was probably the start of our rowing, and for me, the realisation that this definitely was not going to work out.

What started as a discussion just ended up with us bawling at each other, and I could literally feel my blood boiling with anger. I'm not sure if I was annoyed with him or angrier with myself for not waking up to the sort of relationship we actually had. It appeared that he had more important things to do than row with me, and our unproductive slanging match resulted in him stomping out of my flat. This enraged me further. We hadn't resolved a single issue. Then he had the audacity to make his escape in my company car. What a complete tosser! At this point, I realised that the relationship was over for a second and final time, but I still had unfinished business. I needed an outlet for my anger.

I forgot to mention that he did have a couple of hobbies. He loved buying nice expensive shirts, playing football in the Sunday league and eating spicy curries. It was a sort of laddish cult to be able to stomach the hottest curry and to keep a toilet roll in the freezer for the next day. It was his love of spicy food that prompted me to create something special just for him using all of his favourite ingredients. Lots of spices and lots of shirts.

I put the plug in the bath and turned on the tap before popping to the wardrobe to remove his collection of beautifully ironed shirts. Now I know there are women out there who like to cut things up, but having grown up with absolutely nothing, this was a step too far, and I couldn't bear the waste. Once the shirts were covered with water, I retrieved his favourite sauces, spices, and of course, a wooden spoon, from the kitchen. Oh, it was joyous! My anger was instantly transformed into laughter. I mock-asked him if he wanted more red sauce as I dolloped it all over his clothes. Then in with the spices and a really good stir to get everything properly coated. When I sat on the bathroom floor, admiring my work, I knew my anger was spent, but I had a nagging sense that I needed to do more. I suspected that he'd go straight to his favourite haunt, avoid me all night and then return in my car the next day to collect his football kit. I went into the bedroom, and sure enough, there was his kit all ready for the big match the next day. I didn't want to ruin his chances of playing altogether, after all, I wanted him gone for good, and he did fare better with routine. I pondered for a minute or so. Then it came to me: I went back into the kitchen, found myself some scissors and snipped through his football boot laces. Now that felt like a job well done. Basking in the euphoria of my project, I poured myself a glass of white and flicked on the TV.

I was up early the next morning, eager to peer out of the top-floor window and smile as I saw him parking. As predicted, he'd returned just in time to collect his kit. He placed the car keys on the side as he came through the door, and I instantly picked them up. I put them in my pocket and waited for the drama to unfold. First of all, he spotted his clothes in the bath. Much to my surprise, he thought it was hilarious.

Although I was disappointed, it didn't last too long, because when he went to recover his boots, even though I thought this was the lesser of the two offences, he was absolutely furious. Not only was he going to be late for football, but the lads would know. Yes, there it was, the dent to his pride. That's what pushed him over the edge. As he trotted down the stairs with a bag full of dripping, wet, spicy clothes, I knew it was time for a new chapter.

It is interesting that anger and pride are close on the emotional scale, as threats to our pride or standing can trigger anger, but anger can also stem from fear. One of the most common examples I come across is getting cut up in traffic. When Alan joined our weekly meditation group, he said there were two things that made him angry. The first was that no one else in the house would get up to feed the cat. The second was getting cut up in traffic. Our instinct to feel under threat when someone pulls out in front of us is valid because of the obvious dangers associated with car crashes. However, when the danger subsides, quite often our anger doesn't. I asked Alan to imagine his nemesis waking up in the morning, having his coffee and then checking his watch, saying to himself, "If I leave the house now, I'll be just in time to cut in front of Alan at the corner of The Strand and James Street." Depicted in this way, our response seems irrational and yet the experience feels so personal. We develop a relationship with the driver that doesn't actually exist. In this imaginary connection, the driver has deliberately disrespected us and threatened our position in the tribe. We know it's a mind-generated story when the model of car they drive and how they look impacts how we feel about them. Particular brands of car lead us to assume that it is the driver's sense of their own superiority that gives them the right to think that they can push in front. Drivers of less affluent brands have cut us up because they're inferior and probably stupid. We'll even resort to criticising their ability based on their sex, age or hair colour. We don't know anything about this person or their state of mind. They could be responding to an emergency call, on the way to see a sick child, or just wrapped up in the adrenaline of being late.

Once the initial threat has been avoided, it's the stories and assumptions that stoke up our anger. Yet it's a story we don't need to play out. The thoughts and content that follow serve only to prolong our irritation. We are no longer protecting ourselves from real life or death, but saving our pride and our ego from something that only occurred in our minds.

Defending our ego is our life's work as we strive to protect that sense of who we need to be, often confused with who we actually are.

Singing Badly on Karaoke

If you have interpreted from the title that there's a bar and a few large reds involved in this story, then you're very perceptive, but let's not rush into this.

Let's begin the chapter with the wisdom of Eckhart Tolle (2011), who says that, *'We are never upset for the reasons we think.'* It's so easy to observe how our anger ramps up the story, and we personalise a completely random event, such as being cut up in traffic. The brain scans for a response to the situation. When our reaction is disproportionate to the event, it's usually an indication that we're dealing with something deeper. This depth comes from that innate need to self-protect, yet even when the immediate danger subsides, it seems to leave a wound that prolongs the experience.

The overwhelming desire to defend ourselves can lead us down the same patterns of reaction again and again. In the car story, there's a sense of being outdone, pushed to the back of the line and disrespected. It's a threat to our pride, a powerful emotion that can motivate us to achieve greatness. It's an emotion that we should treat with caution, as it can be attached to a sense of status or hierarchy that topples as soon as we become aware of someone we perceive as better in some way. Yet we recognise that there are some areas of our lives where our lack of ability just doesn't bother us. I made my peace with not being great at sports a long time ago. I know I'll never achieve Sports Woman of the Year. When the least athletic kid in the class ran past me, still swinging his arm around in a complete circle, I knew that my fate as an athlete had been sealed. I'd always suspected that sport wasn't really my bag. It had nothing to do with the humiliation of being made to do physical education in our underwear when we forgot our kits. The struggle was always running out of breath. I firmly believe that every mountain should have a Costa coffee halfway up, just so I have an excuse to sit down moments before I reach the stage of requiring actual resuscitation.

I believe we all have strengths, even if we are not bold enough to take them out of the closet. Mine have always been singing and intelligence. I was told from an early age that these two gifts would take me through life to claim the successes that were already written in the stars. When I turned up to the corporate world with my intelligence and work ethic, I thought everything would fall into place. I was ambitious and within weeks of joining a large company, I set myself a target of reaching the next grade within two years. This promotion had taken some people nearly ten years to achieve, but I never let facts get in the way of a good success story. I went over and above taking on more and more responsibility, as if performing the role as advertised wasn't enough. The additional effort I initially offered through choice became an expectation, and this completely flipped my motivation. The harder it became to achieve that elusive promotion, the more resentful I was, particularly towards the manager I felt had none of the ability but all of the kudos associated with the grade and the salary.

With hindsight and many conversations with friends who still find themselves in this position, I realise that when you work for a weak leader, your efforts are often used to fill the gap in their own competencies. It takes a strong person to allow another to shine, when there's a risk it highlights their own failings. Taking full responsibility for my own part in the pantomime, I could have found myself a mentor to help me navigate the landscape and impart a little realism into my plans. Instead of taking on extra projects, believing I could prove myself and get noticed, I could have invested my time strategically, setting firm career goals in conjunction with a mentor I respected, someone who had trodden the path. On reflection, I was too proud. Herein lies the perfect example of how our pride can motivate us to do better, but can also stand in our way. Well, at least I had my singing, and that would come in handy when I set up my arts and music coffee shop.

When I work with retreat customers, we ease ourselves into the day, and there's more opportunity for people to open up and relax. We tend to get the best version of everyone who attends, after all, they're there to switch off the woes of the outside world and take some much-needed time out. This is the version of me I thought would show up to run my coffee shop. It turned out to be a tough gig, and on less than minimum wage, it wasn't the dream job I thought it would be. I really struggled to tolerate some of the customers who found their way into the shop.

They'd ask for half a sandwich or half a piece of cake. The ludicrousness of the request would melt my brain. I wondered who they thought I would sell the other half of their sandwich to. On one occasion, a lady plonked her elbow onto the counter, demanding a glass of water. I handed this to her and she drank it and chatted as she paced up and down on the other side of the counter, observing me like an object of prey. She then asked for another, and when I summoned my politest voice and reminded her that this was, in fact, a business, her response was that water was free.

FREE! I thought, as I mentally collected my soapbox from under the counter. *I'll tell her!* And I did tell her. I gave her a blow-by-blow account of the journey that 350ml of water had made to arrive in her glass, completely free of charge. The purchase of the glass to hold it, the water rates and the washing up liquid. It should have been enough but I was on a roll. I was channelling the Oscar performance of John Cleese and was not going to stop short of a full five-minute rhetoric. I continued with the source of the tiles on which she marched up and down, and the lights over her head powered by free electricity. She didn't go down without a fight, insisting that she might be ill and therefore in need of water. I wondered if she might take ill quite suddenly if she didn't leave my shop very quickly, and calmly asked her to leave. When she was gone, I wondered about her for several hours. She hadn't appeared to be ill and had arrived with a sense of entitlement, which was possibly the cause of my unearthing the entire wrath of my being. Luckily for all involved, not every annoying person in the world made it through the door to the coffee shop, as my faithful assistant Laura once pointed out.

I'd fallen in love with the coffee shop space immediately. It was an old locksmith's across the road from a church. It was on a circular set of buildings known as the quadrant and had huge, almost floor-to-ceiling windows. The entrance was via a gated porchway between the coffee shop and the shop next door. Within the porch, there were the two shop doors and a door to the upstairs flats. When you peered through the glass door on the right, you could clearly see the coffee shop beyond. When my faithful assistant told me that someone had complained that the entrance wasn't clear enough, I swiftly told her that if there were people out there who couldn't find their way through the door, then I certainly didn't want them popping into the shop to annoy me.

What was I worried about? Growing up, I was told that I didn't suffer fools gladly but it doesn't come from a point of extreme intelligence or common sense. Only the other day, I drove the wrong way into the car wash. As I reversed out onto the busy road, dodging the oncoming traffic, I was able to take full responsibility for my actions and to laugh at the comic effect of arriving at the front of the queue, facing the wrong way. We all behave foolishly or take the wrong steps, but I won't take responsibility for something I cannot change, whilst someone else takes no responsibility for their capacity to think. It turns out that running a customer-facing business just wasn't for me, and for the safety of the public, being in an office where I could abuse one person at a time seemed like a much safer option for all involved.

Years later, I worked with a computer programmer who had previously run a pub with his wife. I could imagine him captivating the room, sharing his knowledge and opinions with the crowd. I envisaged him really stepping into the kudos of being the local pub landlord. However, in his own words, he was very bad at dealing with customer complaints. Whilst his wife was despatched to handle the customer, he said he would seethe quietly in the back room. I loved his ability to laugh at himself. When we have a level of self-awareness, we're able to observe our behaviour and have some fun with these tantrums that seem to come from nowhere. Dealing with lots of different customers can make life unpredictable, and as humans, we struggle with uncertainty. But what is there to fear? Life has taught me that I do not fear the behaviour of others as much as I fear how I will react, and when I react, how will I be seen?

How we are seen can be the crux of our struggle with ourselves. I said my strengths were intelligence and singing, but what I didn't explain was my attachment to these traits. I was praised, admired and in my own interpretation, conditionally loved because of these attributes. They became my self-worth, and when things went to plan, I was proud. When they didn't, I was completely unlovable. This isn't a statement of fact but an illustration of how our mind perceives our existence. We build a sense of who we are by examining the behaviours of those we love or admire to work out what pleases them and impresses them. Through this, we strive to create our own image of what that success looks like. This is our crafted self, our ego. It holds the rule book of how we should look and behave, and we spend our lifetime attempting to live up to its expectations and defending its honour when others accuse us of falling short.

When we're born, we can only be who we are. Yet somewhere along the way, we fall out of love with who we really are, believing we're not good enough to show up to the world in that way. We devise ways to make ourselves more loveable, because it keeps us safe. We need to be loved and to belong in order to survive. The difference between who we are and who we think we should be becomes our life's work. In his book *Anxiety*, Smail (2015) suggests that disguising the gap between the two personas is the root cause of our anxiety. The higher the stakes, the greater the fall, and we all know the biggest falls occur on the karaoke stage.

There's an irony in my mum's message to the six-year-old me, happily singing away on the bus. "No one wants to hear you sing!" I think she meant that the bus wasn't really the time or the place. Maybe because of her own childhood experience, she bought into the story that children should be seen and not heard. Yet, many in the world can experience joy through the voice of a happy child.

As it transpired that I could actually sing and write songs, this became my showpiece. My mum would proudly talk about me knowing the words to numerous songs. When my cousins picked something I didn't know, I'd be toppled off my little pedestal. Mostly, I enjoyed sitting on my bed with the guitar learning new songs, and later I loved being in recording studios. It was in these spaces that I got fully immersed in the music and got a true sense of music coming through me. It could feel like an out-of-body experience where I channelled music, a term I've come to know as 'through me', not 'by me'.

I was encouraged to perform. I did so apologetically, always with that nagging doubt that people were just being polite, after all, no one really wanted to hear me sing. The hundreds of compliments and even hypnotism have not shifted that inner lack of confidence because until recently, that one comment has been a lurker. An innocent comment that I filed in my memory bank that didn't reveal itself, but influenced how I felt about singing in public. Now that it's out in the open, I can challenge its power of destruction. Yet the stakes of performance are still high. There are only two things getting me on the karaoke stage. The first is a well-rehearsed song that I know I can perform well; the second is the invincible cloak that only copious amounts of red wine can provide.

Somewhere in my ego, the story of who I am as a person contains a line about a good singer. This random audience that stands before me in the pub knows nothing about keys or vocal ranges. Within an instant, a bad song choice can take away everything that I am.

This is the crux of attaching our traits to our sense of who we are. If we do not feel that we are loved unconditionally, then whatever we are loved for gives us our sense of safety, and therefore, we'll protect it at all costs. When I left my career to open a coffee shop, I learnt quite quickly that my career didn't define me. It wasn't a deep and spiritual realisation, but was forced on me, because if I was my career, then who was I now?

We don't define someone by a broken leg because we know that it isn't who that person is. We recognise the temporary nature of the injury. Yet our sense of self becomes our life raft, we become attached to our roles in society like there are no other roles we could play. By our very nature, we play several roles every day, so isn't it likely that some will drop to make way for others. When we recognise these situations as roles, is it possible to perceive that they don't define who we really are? Separating ourselves from a physical injury or even a role and coming to see ourselves as something bigger is where we begin to challenge that sense of who we are. Who is driving that self-image? On the one hand, it might be our perception of how people see us, or how we see ourselves. But the source of the creation is still the same—the mind.

Our mind is the greatest creator of all, filling our heads with thoughts moment by moment. These thoughts are perceptions of what is happening based on our best guess with the information we can quickly assimilate in a split second. However, we do not recognise this guesswork, treating everything the mind sends us as the ultimate truth. If you think this is risky as an adult, imagine how uninformed it was as a child. Yet it is the child who begins to craft this sense of self that we take into the world.

We create our experience of the world moment to moment based on our interpretation of how similar the current experience is to something we have seen before. Our split-second reaction is measured by our ego to assess how we compare to that crafted sense of self. Yet, we are everything and nothing all at the same time. Our true power comes from knowing that there is no single thing that defines us. The miracle of our human creation is enough. We do not have to collect life loyalty points to have worth in this world. We live in a culture that only measures success financially, promoting individual achievements at the expense of building caring communities. My coffee shop brought together strangers over a pot of tea. Artists and musicians shared their work in an informal, inclusive setting. The locksmiths that once was there gone forever, and even though it has passed through many hands, twenty years later, it is still the coffee shop that I converted all of those years ago.

When we fail, we get a sense that we haven't quite measured up to who we thought we were. We can also fail because we imagine that other people are thinking that we haven't quite measured up to who they thought we were. This is complicated! Yet, where do the criteria for success come from? Is it relevant or contrived because the great novelty of realising that you created yourself in your own image of perfection is realising that everyone else did the same? We're all wandering around trying to live up to this fictional character that we created to keep ourselves safe in the world. Even if we were able to define success, what percentage of the factors that contribute to our success our within our control?

Fear of failure can be debilitating. Yet it's a dark and sneaky emotion that's difficult to quantify. As our ego strives to keep us safe, it is this very fear that can stop us from moving forward. It's difficult to shift, but before we can even fail, we need to define what success looks like. Maybe it's here that we channel our energies. Focusing on what could happen if it went well. Just as a single talent cannot define us, neither can a single transaction. Whatever direction we take, we learn if we are open enough to do so and if we are able to enjoy the steps along the way. We are very quick to bury our successes, but always able to remember those failures because it is those situations that challenge us, that really help us to learn and grow. They stick with us because they were difficult, and yet we overcame.

Whether we are the clever one, pretty one, or kind one, when these traits are glued into our self-worth, the stakes will feel higher than ever. Once we can see them as only a part of who we are, we can begin to shift the weight of them a little, but it won't be a rational shift; it will be something we feel. When I stood up to sing one of my favourite songs ever, it completely bombed. 'Just One More Try' seemed like the easiest song in the world when performed by George Michael. I've sung along to it many times and it's well within my vocal range, yet here I was standing on stage, sounding like an out-of-tune mouse. There weren't many people to witness this catastrophe, but it only really mattered to me. It only mattered that I had let go of my hang-ups, and here, for the first time in my life, I was happy, amused even, not to take myself too seriously. Here I was singing badly on karaoke and learning to enjoy every minute. I wonder if happiness is directly related to the absence of fear because if we can build a contentment that can co-exist with our fears, we are truly unstoppable. This gift is available to us all through a non-judgemental style of self-awareness. It's a capacity to be with our experience as it is. However, that shows up for us.

Sometimes we need to fail to build our resilience. Sometimes we need to fail to know we'll survive. Those who are out there failing with you will understand. It is your choice whether you play it safe or move forward. You may think that those who are observing from the comfort of their safety zones will never understand, but how do we know that they are not looking on in admiration? How do we know that your version of the 'safe' zone was in fact their 'fear of failure' zone?

To ease our move forward, we need a sense of letting go of that character that we've protected for so long, or at least being curious about what it stands for. On the Hawkins scale of emotional energies, pride is right at the top, just below courage. I believe it's because letting go of the great weight that comes with pride moves us from a fear-based approach to prop up our ego to a life spent serving the greater good. I'm not saying that proud people cannot serve the greater good because our energy levels fluctuate between so many different emotions. Unacknowledged pride can get in our way because it can keep us strongly embedded in our ego. It is the humility to break this down that begins our path of true, authentic transformation.

My Little Narcissist

If the ideal sense of who we are is a collection of rules and beliefs, then the ego is the prefect standing guard to defend our honour from external threats. It continually measures our progress against those preconceived ideas, unleashing the harsh voice of the inner critic to get us back on track. The ego builds the walls and battens down the hatches to keep us safe, but the fear of not quite living up to our expectations can keep us trapped, unable to move forward. We're all ego-driven to an extent, but with awareness, we're able to look beyond our own interests and consider the greater good. An extreme form of a self-obsessive ego is the narcissist.

Narcissism was named after the Greek mythological figure, Narcissus, who fell in love with the sight of his own reflection. Yet, my observation of narcissism is that we confuse self-entitlement with self-love. When we learn to love and accept ourselves unconditionally, we build a resilience independent of external validation. The narcissist's constant drive for attention suggests they're unable to provide this contentment for themselves. It's as if their very survival is dependent on them being at the top of the tribal tree, better and stronger than everyone else. They'll go to great lengths to maintain their lofty position, an obsession that underpins many of their traits. As the perceived leader of the tribe, they expect to be the centre of the universe, constantly engineering ways they can make this happen. When they're expected to turn up as a member of the supporting cast, they often won't be able to make it. Extreme personalities will project their absence back onto the host, suggesting they've done something that makes the narcissist's attendance untenable. Assessing themselves as the strongest member of the tribe, the narcissist must continually assert themselves. They're not afraid to instigate the type of confrontation that most of us avoid. Their behaviour becomes repellent and leaves people feeling on edge, causing them to be excluded from social gatherings. Unfortunately, being left out dents their fragile ego, triggering more aggressive behaviour. Their comfort with confrontation leaves us feeling apprehensive of being physically harmed. Yet, even the physically weaker narcissist can wield their power because psychologically they know how to expose us to the disempowering feelings of guilt and shame. Even if we fight back, the remorse of losing our temper, particularly around someone who is vulnerable, leads us straight back to the feelings of shame and guilt. We might interpret this as emotional astuteness on behalf of the narcissist. Perhaps it's their own permanent struggle with shame and guilt that makes them so familiar with these emotions. We might detect a hint of this transference when the narcissist tells us our opinion because they're usually projecting their own views onto us.

The narcissist can never be wrong. When their obnoxious behaviour is challenged, they'll deny the facts even when it seems so obvious to everyone else. If denial doesn't work, they may admit that the behaviour took place, but not in the way everyone else remembers.

When lying and denial don't work, they'll admit that the behaviour occurred, but that the victim overreacted. Once the seeds of confusion have been planted, the narcissist's trump card is to make themselves the victim of the entire event. Before we know it, it's no longer about them upsetting someone else, but back to their favourite topic of discussion, themselves. Once the narcissist has claimed the victim prize, it's now up to us to make amends for our actions. Over time, they'll forgive us and bestow the honour of allowing us back into their inner sanctuary. We're so relieved that the conflict has been resolved, but we're left wondering what the hell happened. Often, we'll find ourselves on guard because the narcissist doesn't recognise our personal boundaries. They appear to take great joy from the power of putting others back into their rightful place, privately and publicly.

It's not always easy to spot the narcissist as they switch between charm and challenge, leaving us feeling just a little bit confused about the relationship. The most poignant way to describe their antics is cloudy. The compliment laced with an insult, "Oh, that outfit looks much better on you than the one you wore yesterday," leaves you wondering whether you've been praised or attacked. The wording is so subtle that retaliation looks petty or oversensitive. Once we've been on the negative side of their behaviour a few times, most of us alter our approach. We find ourselves walking on eggshells, trying to predict the physical and emotional attack, avoid treading on their ego or poised for the breach of our emotional boundaries. Yet, even when we tread the path of least resistance, we can never predict the comment that will dent the narcissist's ego and incur their wrath once again. If we're too successful, they might sense our caution and turn up their charm once again, leaving us to believe we have imagined the entire thing, only to swoop in when we let down our guard. It's not personal, *'confusion weaves an intricate tapestry of cognitive dissonance and emotional turmoil'*, Neurolaunch.com (2024).

It's difficult to imagine how strong, sane and well-adjusted individuals succumb to a level of control that can leave them feeling angry, despondent, disengaged, disempowered and helpless. Helplessness can seep into every area of our lives, stripping us of the energy we need to fight back. Most of us wouldn't tolerate such a damaging relationship, but the narcissist never shows their hand. Being on the wrong side of narcissism is like being part of a delicious recipe in a slow cooker. It starts with all of the right ingredients, but as it heats up, they're replaced with toxins. Narcissists don't introduce themselves in all of their glory but stalk around the edges, watching and assessing our usefulness. We are then 'chosen' in some way, and they know how to make us feel special and seen. The more vulnerable we are, the more they're able to tap into those feelings of invisibility. We become the glitzy, adored possession, the Gucci bag. We're the status symbol the narcissist craves, but we must be careful not to shine too brightly, as we're there to live in the shadows of the narcissist and mustn't trigger their insecurities.

The initial love and flattery they offer lure us into this seemingly normal, equal relationship. Against this backdrop, we become exposed to two forms of cognitive dissonance. The first is their ever-changing behaviour, which leaves us confused about what's going on; the second is the trust in our own instinct. We cannot believe this person is anything other than our original assessment and find it difficult to accept that our instinct to identify friend or foe is flawed, because where would that leave us? Once the relationship is established, the destruction begins, a gradual stripping away of our strengths combined with subtle steps to isolate us from those we love. Gradually, our faith in ourselves becomes weaker until we feel completely helpless and trapped.

We can be lured into a toxic relationship, but it's easier to be captured when we've already been trained. When we're familiar with the narcissist dance, as toxic as it is, it feels like our sense of normal. It's a pattern that we recognise. I started my training when I was three or four years old. A close family relative stepping in as a father figure already had the control box ticked. I couldn't rationalise the relationship at that age; instead, I felt it, as children do. Arnold was the doting hero who rushed in to save the day, but I could see the shadow. It reminded me of the Pink Panther sketch where the cartoon character wanders around all day trying to outwit a rain cloud. I could sense the temperature before a word was spoken. The morning anger and volatility, the fun and games after a couple of drinks and then the tipping point. He'd talk at me for hours, offloading his sadness and woes. I was frozen in time without the emotional vocabulary or courage to remove myself from his fragile ego, trying to get all of the responses correct, to keep him on an even keel. When he moved on, I was the eight-year-old child who walked to the phone box once a week, to ring him and check he was okay. I stayed over the odd weekend to keep him company. I have fond memories of learning to make trifle and singing along to his records. Despite the challenges of his unpredictable behaviour, there was a part of me who also saw his vulnerability, a deep, sad hole that could never be filled. It would take me many years to realise that this was not a problem I could solve, but oh, how I tried. How I wanted to just make his pain go away. It never occurred to me that this wasn't my responsibility, even when a very astute counsellor asked me a probing question.

I hadn't chosen to go to a counsellor; I'd been accused of lying and was facing expulsion from college. When I left home to go to music college at the age of sixteen, it was natural that I saw less of my family. I was at college during the week and had a Saturday job in McDonald's, so I reduced my visits to Arnold to about one per month. He was settled and seemed happy with his partner of eight years, so I was deeply saddened when one Friday evening, he told me that he was seriously ill. I was obviously distressed and didn't want to pry into the details, but it was clear from his words that it was terminal, and he didn't have long left.

Getting a place at music college had been a difficult process. Many people, including my high school music teacher, had fought my corner. I couldn't give it up, but I knew that if I could restructure my Friday lectures, I could probably visit Arnold at least once per week after college. From 10am to 4.30pm on Fridays, I had no lectures. I was a violin player, and at 4.30pm, the string players attended a practice session for an hour. None of us wanted to go because it was right at the end of the day and interfered with our weekends. So, when I spoke to the head of the department about Arnold's circumstances, he was very understanding and allowed me to miss the sessions. My best friend, also a string player, was furious because she still had to attend.

I have no idea how it all unravelled. I suspect it was a casual conversation between myself and my friend when she enquired after Arnold's health. I didn't have many details and probably answered vaguely that he seemed to be okay. He never said he was cured or that the illness had gone, but it's not an easy subject to raise. How do you ask someone why they're still alive? My friend thought the entire thing was unbelievable and marched off to the head, accusing me of lying. The college staff were appalled that I was the sort of person who would pretend someone was dying just to get out of a class. I had two options: leave college or speak to a counsellor. So here I was sitting, talking to the counsellor, fending off my imminent expulsion. Whilst I was initially apprehensive about the interrogation, I came to enjoy our conversations, but I couldn't see how our chats would really turn around the college's decision, after all, they just didn't believe my version of events. Yet, I still remember the question that turned everything around. In our third session, the counsellor asked me whether I thought it was my responsibility to look after my parents. Without giving it a second thought, I said I did. Whilst I thought I was absolutely right and she now understood my predicament, I realise now that I had things the wrong way around. My answer had given her an insight into the dynamics of home life and how embedded my false beliefs were. She didn't ask to see me again, and when I returned to college, the staff seemed a little nicer.

Our lived experience is complex, and it can be all that we know. Did I have any idea what narcissism was in the 1980s? Did I understand the dynamics of parenting? I knew I was absolutely firm in my views and interpretation of the world. I had my version of normal. When we begin to grow, we start to open up to the concept that our thoughts and beliefs may not be as solid as they first appear. We come into contact with people who have a lived experience that is entirely different to ours and is as real and as solid for them as our own is. It can be complex to bring our beliefs out into the open as they're an unquestionable part of who we believe ourselves to be. Narcissism shines a light on the extreme nature of our actions; we all have egos and are all susceptible to ego-based behaviours. As the narcissist fights with the world to uphold their ego, we also fight to uphold our own, albeit a less self-absorbed version.

It's not the ego that is our ultimate challenge, but our tendency to hold it as the ultimate truth of who we are. Through self-awareness, we can gently explore letting go of this solid sense of self, but it's tough to let go of what's familiar. Yet, setting an intention to challenge who we think we are, whether deliberate or not, is the starting point to realising authentic liberation. It requires courage, which is why Hawkins (2013) describes courage as the pivotal point in our transformational growth.

Turning the Evolutional Corner

'The definition of insanity is repeating the same mistakes and expecting a different result.' Unknown.

Hindsight's a gift, and I could use it to give many examples of behaviours and reactions that led me straight down the road to burn out, but here's the thing. By its definition, a pattern can only be created through repetition. As for mistakes, we probably recognise them when things go wrong. We don't make them intentionally.

When I found myself crying on the loo at my coffee shop, all of that initial excitement completely diminished. Was that an exhaustion pattern? Isn't working ridiculous hours with no time off for very little money, enough to push anyone over the edge? Had I expected too much from myself or underestimated the task in hand? Absolutely, but this could be explained away by a lack of experience. Work history can be complex. For me, working for a demanding small business, a role in a corporate IT department and setting up a coffee shop business were all challenging for different reasons. Looking at our environments to identify the root causes of burnout becomes impossible, and yet it's often where we start when we're washed out with exhaustion. We attempt to resolve the feelings we have inside by trying to correct what's happening on the outside. This can be valid, but how can we truly know our experience without understanding what's happening within us? How do we identify the root causes that take us down a particular emotional road?

My coffee shop didn't deliver the freedom or peace of mind I'd expected, so I returned to my original role in IT, where I'd started my career fifteen years earlier. A year later, I reluctantly closed down my coffee shop venture. The staff were disappointed but didn't appreciate that after working a forty-hour week in IT, I couldn't face working in the café on Saturdays for free. I brought a mix of skills to the IT role, spreading my time across consultancy, analysis, software testing and project management. It was an interesting time, particularly as the company was expanding, so I got to travel to glamourous places such as Dubai, Paris and Mauritius. I could leave that image of success right there, but the trips provided limited opportunities for sightseeing. In Mauritius, I barely got past the airport shop where I was staff training, and after working two fifteen-hour days on the trot, I was physically shaking when I got back to my hotel room on the second night. These hours were unusual, as the company's typical working pattern was 9 – 5.30, but as the team was scaled back, those of us remaining were under pressure to take on more responsibilities. Six years in, and I found myself stressed and physically exhausted. Workplace burnout is a recent phenomenon, World Health Organisation (2019), so at that time, I was diagnosed with depression and took a month off. Some days, I just couldn't face getting out of bed; my body felt so physically heavy. This was also my safety zone where I could hide away, and there were no demands on me. I was troubled by the fear that maybe I just couldn't hold down a role and my mind would wander down that rabbit hole of losing my job, my home and how I'd be judged. When we're absolutely worn out, the last thing we need is inner judgement, but the mind cannot help itself. A year after being ill, I was made redundant.

I could see the pathway to redundancy being carved out for me. I felt it creeping towards me. When it came to responsibilities, the company adopted vague job roles and titles because they provided ultimate flexibility and yet my manager had started to home in on my official job title. It was a management title that could easily be justified as not being required, but it didn't acknowledge the range of skills I provided. It was very painful to have my contribution and commitment marginalised in this way.

A few weeks earlier, my manager had hinted that I should look for another role. I knew I'd fallen from grace when he told me that he'd previously believed that should the company scale back to a minimum, he and I could run it between the two of us. That one comment told me everything I needed to know. He wasn't talking about a partnership, but an arrangement where he did what he wanted, and I picked up everything else. There was no consideration for any aspirations I might have. One Monday morning, we were all invited to a meeting to explain the redundancy process, and on Friday of the same week, I left.

When I found contracting a few months later, I entered a market where my skills were valued and soon built up a network of contacts who'd invite me to work on projects as and when they were available. This flexibility became a true gift when I started studying and building up my mindfulness business. I'd had a lifelong interest in the mind and qualified as an NLP practitioner and life coach, but the courses didn't quench my thirst to understand human nature. I began unlocking this great mystery by accident during an episode of Inspector Morse. I'd spent the 1990s living in Oxford and loved watching Morse and identifying the familiar places. When I meet people for the first time, I often drop hints about my time at Oxford, laughing when they take the bait and imagine I studied there. Whilst I was daydreaming of my non-existent Oxford degree, I wondered whether there was ever a universe in which their demand for mature students might motivate them to lower the entry criteria, so people like me could sneak in through the back door. *Well,* I thought, *there's no harm in finding out,* as I used my little fudge fingers to tap NLP into the search bar. I'd never heard of mindfulness and was intrigued when it came up as a master's degree option. The prospectus looked fascinating, but the entrance criteria was clinical. Never one to let the lack of skills or qualifications hold me back, I instantly searched for other universities and came across Bangor University. They didn't require clinical experience but attendance on their eight-week stress reduction course. Wow, did I need that. I booked on straight away, mentally ticking 2018 resolutions off my list. That's how I came to be travelling along the A55 to Bangor on a cold January evening. These night classes were serious business; I'd tell my husband as I set off with a blanket and my favourite cushion. It was absolute bliss. I cannot think of anything kinder for the stressed mind than lying under a blanket following a soothing, guiding body scan. Coming from a corporate background, it felt very odd to be lying on the floor with a group of twenty-two strangers, but in a way, the weirdness made it fun. This was also our homework, and I was three weeks into this practice when I had a profound experience. After finishing the daily body scan, I walked into the kitchen and stopped dead in my tracks as I realised that my mind was completely still. The wheel of continuous churning thoughts wasn't turning. I was eager to learn more but reluctant to commit to a five-year master's programme. More research led to a three-year format at Aberdeen University that included taught weekend retreats at a monastery in Scotland and annual retreats to Holy Isle off the West Coast of Arran. It sounded idyllic. Just like the stress course, the master's was experiential but also delved into the science of mindfulness and neuroscience. As I learnt about the complexity of our thoughts and emotions, I began to wonder if I wasn't broken after all. These minds of ours are complicated, and when our thoughts arise, they're already accompanied by heavy emotions, Choden & Regan-Addis (2017), that can leave us drowning in an emotional turmoil. Our energy levels align with our emotions, so drifting from one feeling to another can be uplifting or draining.

The most comprehensive explanation of how emotions impact our energy levels comes from Hawkins (2013), who has mapped our emotions to the energetic feeling we experience. He puts our lived experience into context, challenging our understanding of energy only relating to the calories we consume. However, if our food, sleep patterns and exercise regime remained constant for seven days, would we feel the same each day? Would we have the same amount of energy? We can start the day feeling buoyant, but our interactions with others can sometimes dampen our spirit. Damasio (2000) states that *'we think we are logical beings that feel, but we are emotional beings that think.'* Motivation, a high-energy feeling, doesn't come from eating carrots. Hawkins defines energy in motion, E-MOTION and my yoga teacher reminds me that energy is ever present. The vibration of that energy is expressed as an emotion. Hawkins allocates a numeric frequency to each of our emotions, much like musical notes have their own vibrational frequency. The numbers in the scale provide context to illustrate how our energetic emotions relate to each other. They should not be taken literally. The first set is described as fear-based emotions ranging from the demobilising energy of shame up to the stronger emotion of courage:

20 Shame
30 Guilt
50 Apathy
75 Grief
100 Fear
125 Desire
150 Anger
175 Pride
200 Courage

Note that the energy of shame has the lowest number. Whereas the vibrational energy of courage is ten times as powerful. Hawkins describes courage as the turning point in our transformation. We've explored the withdrawal energy of shame; the guilt that leaves us feeling that we haven't lived up to expectations and the complete apathy of shutting down. It's grief that perhaps highlights how our energy fluctuates from the slow pace of apathy to the power of anger at the opposite end of the spectrum. There's a palpable power in anger that's absent from apathy. It's the energy of anger that can give us the strength to move through grief. Similarly, fear moves along a continuum between the freeze response of apathy and the fight response of anger. Our emotional path isn't linear. We don't progress to courage remaining there indefinitely; we learn to ride the unpredictable emotional roller-coaster.

Like a game of snakes and ladders, we might be on an even keel only to be triggered by an experience or thought that takes us back down the snake to apathy.

French bread is my apathy. Growing up in the 1980s, French breadsticks were a novelty only available in some supermarkets. Mum shopped at Kwik Save or Iceland, and if we wanted a French stick, we went to Asda in the main town. Originally a frozen food retailer, Iceland continually extended their range until finally French bread made it to their shelves. Mum was very excited by the arrival of the crusty bread, so just to wind her up, I used to pick off the crusty top. It was only when she came to pay that she'd notice the end of the stick was missing. Whenever I see a French stick, it takes me right back to that scene, and I experience happiness and sadness simultaneously. This is emotional snakes and ladders; our emotional state can change in an instant. According to Hawkins (2013), despite having powerful minds, most of us are subservient to our emotions because, as they arise, we respond to them on autopilot. Hawkins (2013) also suggests that for 80% of Americans, these emotions are fear-based. Inspirational speaker Tony Robbins concurs that we all have an emotional setting that we default to under stress.

I imagine the British statistics would match those of America because of our continuous exposure to fear-based news and advertisements all implying that we can't afford to be content as there's always something awful just around the corner. Yet, the reality of human nature is that we're surrounded by acts of kindness within our communities. The media focuses on the grimmest aspects of human nature, feeding a fear-based rhetoric that taps into our tribal survival instinct. We can belong to multiple tribes for different reasons—the Covid-19 vaccination was particularly tribal. Both the vaccinated and the unvaccinated considered themselves to be right about completely opposite choices, each seeing the other as having an inferior intellect. Often, when we meet people with opposing views, we imagine they're less informed or make poor decisions due to their comparative lack of intellect. We respond to terror acts on people like us more compassionately than we do attacks on those of a different race or culture. Somehow, these differences provide a distance that has a shallower draw on our emotions. The triumphs and challenges of our in-laws may seem less significant than those of our close family circle. We forget that they feel as strongly about their experiences as we feel about ours. There can be inter-team conflict in the workplace where it seems acceptable to judge the work of non-team members, like we've received some sort of superiority trophy. A weak leader will align with the team's view to retain their position, whereas a strong leader understands one important and undeniable fact. We are all human and we are all capable of human things, good or bad. Recognising this shared humanity demonstrates a higher level of conscious awareness. It's a willingness to accept our common fallibility, bringing reason and a more neutral attitude to our experiences.

These traits vibrate with a higher energy as we move away from the weight of the fear-based emotions into what Hawkins (2013) describes as the emotional steps towards peace and enlightenment:

200	Courage	400	Reason
250	Neutrality	600	Peace
310	Willingness	700	Enlightenment
350	Acceptance		

The numbers indicate how our energy becomes faster as we move up the scale and literally raise our energetic vibration.

The gateway to this higher energy is courage, typically visualised as a grand gesture, the knight in shining armour making their way onto the battlefield. Instead, it's the small steps we take every day to consider our inner and outer experiences from a place of curiosity. When our five-year-old self witnesses Aunty Mable complimenting Mum on a tidy house, we unwittingly make a decision. Is housekeeping a trait we want to adopt to earn validation from Aunty Mable, or do we refuse to be perceived in the same way deliberately rebelling against the trait? If we're criticised for speaking up, do we learn to keep the peace at the expense of our opinion? When our actions receive praise, does the joy of that experience cause us to embed particular behaviours into our personality so we remain praiseworthy? Both praise and criticism contribute to our definition of what is required of a human being, worthy of their place within the tribe.

Hundreds of these early experiences contribute to a vault of ideas about who we should be, building this identity we know as the ego. That sense of how we want to show up in the world is crafted, and we'll spend a lifetime defending this manufactured identity. After all, if we're not our ego, who are we? Brené Brown refers to this defence strategy as armouring up, presenting ourselves to the world through a protective coat of arms. Author of *Anxiety*, Smail (2015), believes that our deep anxiety is the fear of being seen as we truly are in place of the ego's perfect sense of self. It sounds very much like imposter syndrome, but the resolution is embodied and much deeper than cognitively comprehending a few pointers on a PowerPoint slide. Just as our ego is created through a multitude of small experiences, according to Brené Brown and Glennon Doyle, courage is the small, intentional choices we make every single day. We have the right to choose, but do we have the skills? Hawkins (2013) believes we are continually at the mercy of our emotions and that many of us will not get the opportunity to move much beyond our default state. For Hawkins, transcending our fear-based narrative requires both courage and the skill to bring mindful awareness to our inner and outer worlds.

Mindfulness is more than the ten-minute visualisation at the end of our yoga class, although relaxation is the best place for the stressed mind to start. The University of Aberdeen focuses on three core pillars, mindful awareness, compassion and insight. Beyond relaxation, there's an awareness that allows us to observe our experience in real time. We can't intercept the speed of the alarm system within the amygdala, but in between this limbic reaction and our automated behavioural response, theirs a split-second gap of around fifteen milliseconds which is referred to as the mindful pause.

Once we develop this pause, we no longer react but choose how to respond. As Jon Kabat Zinn suggests, *'We can't hold back the waves but we can learn to surf.'* Mindfulness training develops this ability to pause, and as we do, our awareness of that ego-based identity begins to come into sight. This journey of inner discovery gradually reveals our true self, and it will not live up to the ideals of the ego. This can be difficult to observe in all of its human glory, as we face into our sense of worth. Compassion is the second pillar of mindfulness, and it encourages us to cultivate a safe and supportive attitude towards our experience. It is through compassion that we're able to explore the trickier aspects of our being. Working compassionately with the less favourable sides of our personality guides us towards an acceptance of who we are and an experiential sense of what it is to be human. This naturally awakens compassion for all that walk this human path, taking us into the energies of neutrality, acceptance and finally peace. The third pillar of mindfulness, insight, is a powerful gift from our bodies, the storage unit for all that has gone before. When we're able to sit with our difficult experiences, overcoming the instinctive desire to push them away, the body and mind reveal the original source of our stories. The comments and behaviours that caused us to place the foundational bricks in our sense of self. This is the deep insight that reveals our own true nature and that of humanity.

Once we begin on our mindful discovery, we never go back to a life of non-awareness. Instead, we keep going working with the edges towards a life filled with more joy and compassion. It's a challenge that leads to the uncovering of our authentic, energetic selves, released from the weight of fear-based emotions.

This is your journey of *The Emotional Hustle,* and I'm with you all the way.

Part Two

Sharpening Your Axe

I'd well and truly lost my motivation. As a Mindfulness Association teacher, I've committed to a daily meditation practice, and I'll promote its benefits to anyone who will listen. For a number of years, it aligned with my ambition to teach and gain a master's degree. It felt exciting and new. Unfortunately, that was part of the problem. I'd attached my sense of purpose to a goal I'd achieved and now I was struggling to keep up my daily practice. I was getting on with it, but it was starting to feel more like a necessary chore. I hadn't recognised that my purpose was adrift, but I was about to have an uncomfortable encounter that would spell it out for me.

I'd invested thousands of pounds in the inner MBA course but ironically, we can learn so much about ourselves from simply bumping into those people we find difficult. It was meeting Diana, another student, that gave me the insight I needed. Sounds True host the inner MBA and they're passionate about spreading the word of mindfulness. Their course is in three parts: self-discovery, mindfulness in teams and mindfulness in the workplace. They're prominent in the United States where mindfulness appears to be more integrated into the workplace culture and this was my angle. I wanted to know just how mindfulness had been incorporated into organisations. I was also excited to be learning from inspirational teachers such as Jack Kornfield and Tara Brach. There were just twelve European students amongst the three thousand cohort that had signed up, and when we were encouraged to create a networking group, Diana sought me out.

I still carry a strange belief that everyone I meet already knows that I was the one selected last for the school team events. As this unpopularity label stands out like a beacon, I was intrigued when Diana messaged me. She didn't mess around with informalities, but instantly suggested we work together on the first assignment. Over our first two-hour Zoom meeting she explained how her multi-million-pound business had been adversely impacted by Covid. She had a UK training facility that had dwindled to nothing, and the inner MBA was about refreshing her knowledge and creating new courses she could offer online. Diana was motivated to rebuild her business and I was impressed by what she'd achieved. Whilst I felt empathetic towards her financial challenges, intuitively I felt uneasy in her company. Diana and I were good friends and very alike. I didn't particularly feel this connection, but this was something Diana kept telling me and she definitely had a way of controlling the narrative. Hours of calls in we'd made no progress on the assignment, so I began my own work in the background. Diana kept getting us together and I couldn't really figure out why. When we eventually did discuss the course, Diana admitted that she was enjoying it but was behind on the material. She also hadn't completed any of the recommended mindfulness practices but did make a very telling observation: "80% of the stuff we're learning is related to what you do, isn't it?" she said one evening.

It was, and whilst I'd seen it as professional development, this was all new ground for Diana. I was surprised that she'd made such an investment without really understanding the course content but all of that was irrelevant because Diana had a plan. She was interested in us creating a working partnership. She'd already pitched mindfulness to a couple of her clients and with me on board, I could create the course content, and she could professionally curate it and distribute it to her network. This was an amazing opportunity for me, particularly as one of her clients desperately needed a scalable stress management solution and I'd created one as part of my master's research. Diana was meeting with her client the next day and asked if I could pull together a proposal on how my stress management course could work for her client. It was needed ASAP, so I worked through the evening to create it. I got it over to her for the next morning. I was eager for her feedback but instead I was met with radio silence. After all of that urgency, there was nothing until she resurfaced a few weeks later. Now we needed to have an urgent meeting so once we'd agreed on a time, Diana suggested she would ring me just in case her previous meeting ran over. I waited for her call to come through, but instead I received an email from her personal assistant. Diana was having problems getting through and suggested that I ring her on an alternative number. At the time, it seemed like an insignificant mix-up, but it became typical of the senseless drama that accompanied even the basic interactions. Our relationship developed a predictable ebb and flow. Diana made urgent demands and then disappeared until the next request. I would like to describe her as a difficult customer but absolutely no money changed hands. Still, I hung in there in anticipation of the great opportunities that could come my way and eventually Diana arranged a call between me and her client.

The client was only available on the last working day before Christmas, December 23rd, but it was imperative that they meet me before signing up for my stress management course, Mind21. Diana would be out of the country, but we had a call the day before, and she advised me to stick to the course content and to leave the financials to her. As we'd be working together, Diana requested immediate access to an evaluation copy of Mind21. She was leaving the country that day and intended to follow the first week of the programme, whilst she was on holiday. She needed it set up in the next couple of hours, to test her access before she jetted off. It was a real judgement call, but I did it because I wanted the relationship to work and that required mutual trust. The call with Diana's client went well, and I built up a good rapport with the engineering manager. By the end of December, the partnership with Diana appeared to be in a really good place.

Unfortunately, when January came, Diana was typically difficult to get hold of and had only completed one day of the course.

When we finally met, it was to express her disappointment that the client deal wouldn't go ahead because they still had outstanding questions, and I hadn't got back to them with answers. This was a big deal for me, and I felt physically sick believing that I'd dropped the ball on such an amazing opportunity, particularly as the call had gone so well. I couldn't quite work out what had gone wrong and awash with self-doubt, I checked the email trail, trying to pin down the missing pieces.

As I searched through the correspondence, it dawned on me that everything had gone through Diana. I'd never had the client's contact details. Keen to get back on track, I made various recommendations about how we could rescue the project, but Diana was vague and dismissive, flippantly telling me not to worry about it. It was tough to let go as I don't like letting people down. I also hated feeling judged for something that didn't appear to be my fault. Luckily for me, a few days later, Diana had a new suggestion for getting the client back on side and asked me to travel down to London to run a free lunchtime workshop. This would be an opportunity to showcase my expertise, and I could even stay at her house to reduce my travelling costs. We could use any spare time to work on our partnership. If I'm completely honest, the idea of spending hours together filled me with dread. Having serious doubts about the relationship, I steered the event towards an online lunch and learn.

Meanwhile, I still wanted to get her evaluation of my stress management course. When I support clients through Mind21, it's usual to discuss their experience and what has come up for them, but with Diana, this was a challenge. Highlighting her need to control the narrative, she continually steered the conversation away from her progress. Keeping the discussion on track was difficult, but on the one occasion when we became close to a breakthrough, Diana dropped her little bombshell. She questioned why she should complete the course at all. I was absolutely flabbergasted, angry and offended, after months of jumping to her demands. After all, she'd tracked me down to start this partnership and then requested free access. Now she was asking why. Diana was arguing with her own motives but expecting me to provide the answer. I wasn't sure what to say, but that was irrelevant as Diana continued regardless, "If I wake up at 5am, I can spend thirty minutes following your programme, or I can spend that time working and getting ahead of the day."

Maybe Diana wanted me to get clearer on the 'why' or the benefits. Maybe, she'd genuinely lost sight of what we'd discussed. Either way, her words touched a deep nerve within me. In that one question, she had literally tapped into my own thought process. This was me, driven by a mind that was determined to spend every waking moment occupied by doing. Why would anyone show up to meditate when they could use that time to get ahead of the day, whatever that even means? Wow, if I couldn't answer this for myself, how could I motivate clients to follow a daily practice? I needed to find an answer for her, but also for myself.

Over the next few days, I allowed the question to bob around in my mind, letting go of the desire to obsess or overthink it. The process reminded me of a computer programmer I worked with. He could spend an entire afternoon grappling with a coding problem, but the answer would pop into his head when he was cleaning his teeth. This is a higher wisdom that exists within us all, but it needs space to emerge. It's not the absence of thoughts that creates this space, but the ability to allow our thoughts to come and go without overanalysing or clinging onto them. The answers come when the mind is still.

Diana's answer arrived in the form of a quotation that's often attributed to Abraham Lincoln. "If my life depended upon my ability to cut down a tree in five minutes, I would spend three minutes sharpening my axe." There it was! In those very words, I recognised myself as the tree hacker. I knew without one single doubt that I'd jump straight in with my blunt axe, whacking it against the side of that tree until my time was up. Forget the planning and the preparations, let's just start doing, whether it's the right thing or not. When I decorate, I'm inspired by the transformation, taking something old or tired and magically turning it into something fresh and vibrant. I don't want to spend twenty minutes collecting the materials, followed by an hour of masking up. Being interested in how it looks at the end makes preparation tedious, and it feels like a psychological step backwards. I have to invite my adult into the room to convince myself that good preparation improves the final finish. This is the discipline of that higher wisdom within.

Diana's question demonstrates just how easily the mind drives us on with a sense of urgency that only actually exists in the mind. It can feel very real and even exciting when we get up an hour earlier and fit more things into the day, but we're allowing that axe to roam free and hack at the tree, because we haven't mastered our own mind. This powerful tool drives our behaviours unchallenged by our higher wisdom, because on some level, we believe we are the mind, seeing it as the ultimate truth. Getting ahead of the day is a story we tell ourselves about the number of hours we have to work or the number of things we have to accomplish. The mind continually pushes, driving us on through the fear of not making the cut. Each time we accomplish a task, our hormones reward us, so we become trapped between fear and reward. In this context of doing, pausing to meditate feels counterintuitive. It's a task that we could simply leave off the list. Yet this is exactly how we get to sharpen our axe. We can learn to challenge and navigate these habitual thoughts of not doing or being enough and we need to because these are the very thoughts that drive our emotional energy. In Buddhist wisdom traditions, there's a philosophy: 'You should sit in meditation for twenty minutes per day unless you are particularly busy and then you should sit for an hour.' It is through meditation that we master the tools to navigate *The Emotional Hustle* of life.

After seven years of practice, I still find myself working through my own emotional baggage with no clear visibility of how much there is to do. We can't outrun it and until we unpack it or clear it, it hovers in the shadows, lurking like that menacing grey rain cloud ready to burst open and drown us at any minute. The reality is that many of us are driven by unseen beliefs, and it was only when I began to discover my own that I finally felt like I wasn't broken after all. It took me nearly fifty years to feel okay and left me wondering how many others struggle at the mercy of destructive thoughts and emotions. Holocaust survivor and psychologist Viktor Frankl believes the human soul can overcome the bleakest of conditions when they have a strong sense of purpose. *'Those who have a 'why' to live, can bear with almost any 'how'.'* Frankl (1946). It's my purpose to shine a light on our emotional challenges so we can gently return to who we really are.

This is my 'why' for *The Emotional Hustle.* I never aspired to the dizzy heights of personal transformation, but when we open our hearts and minds to self-discovery, amazing things happen. We gradually come to know the person we were born to be before everything else got in the way.

Through mindfulness, I have a chance to live life at a particular pace, challenging what is real and what is concocted in the mind. Whilst we're all at the mercy of our powerful thoughts, some of us are addicted to the habitual drama that stokes everything up. Diana may have had some great opportunities for my business, but I knew that for my own sanity, the cost of this partnership was too high. I told Diana that Mind21 was about sharpening her axe, just before we parted company.

"Mindfulness Isn't for Everyone!"

It was a beautiful sunny day and Dad and I were having a peaceful walk along the Wirral Way. The twelve-mile route follows the journey of the Hooton to West Kirby train line, which was discontinued in 1962. In parts, it scenically hugs the stunning coast of the Dee estuary with views across to North Wales. At this point in my career, I'd been training in mindfulness for almost five years and was building a coaching business. It had never been my intention to introduce Dad to mindfulness, so I was surprised and bemused when, as if from nowhere, in his usual jovial style, he said, "Mindfulness isn't for everyone!" His observation landed like a well-planned self-defence strategy as if he harboured a deep fear that I'd drag him off to yoga for a soul cleansing. Only the week before, my niece had smudged my brother with cleansing sage, but that had absolutely nothing to do with me, although it made me laugh a lot. In the past, I might have been tempted to introduce him to some of the benefits, but I was on a mission to stop fixing the world. I was learning to become the lighthouse guiding the boats but not rushing out to sea to entice them in.

Mindfulness can be associated with religion, and I know Dad still carries the mental scars from his time in a Catholic convent school. Maybe he was anxious about being indoctrinated into some cult. Whatever his reasons, I got it. I mean, who am I to be standing on my little soapbox telling everyone to meditate? Who indeed! Dad is one of the calmest people I know and literally drifts through life without a care in the world. Maybe he's right. Maybe he's enlightened. Let's leave that there for a minute or two.

For me, it had become a bit of a personal mission. I've endured too many years struggling with self-worth, striving, emotional abuse, stress, depression and anxiety. If it's related to the emotional system, then it's probably on my bingo card. What scares me is that I just assumed that this challenging inner world I'd built for myself was completely normal. I only recognised problems when I reached burnout, an experience I'd endured multiple times before I wondered whether I was broken and why I couldn't cope. I'd never imagined there was any other way to feel or to navigate life. There was just that nagging doubt that things were not quite right. I lived in hope of a miracle cure for whatever malady it was that just stopped me from being happy. I came closest on the yoga mat. Not the moving about bit, but the lying down at the end, sometimes followed by tea and biscuits. I'd always been curious about yoga, but I didn't choose it; in a way, it found me. In an attempt to build an income outside of the corporate world, I'd started selling Herbalife. I loved the products but the promise of part-time hours delivering an income was definitely oversold. I advertised in the local paper and got a call from a yoga teacher who had used the Herbalife products before. When we met up, it turned out that she had one space available in her small Monday evening yoga class. After a few days of mulling it over, I joined up. This was a time when thoughts of my annoying boss seemed to dominate every waking minute, and it was my yoga teacher who told me that meditation would help.

The guided visualisations at the end of her classes always left me feeling calm and relaxed, but I just didn't make the connection with meditation. Whilst she was explaining that I'd find it beneficial, I nodded politely and smiled whilst the rational voice in my head shouted, *What is the point?* What if I meditated for ten minutes every day as she recommended? Even if I managed to pull this off without her guidance, I'd only feel good for those ten minutes and maybe a few minutes after. What about the other twenty-three hours and fifty minutes? I often wonder how different life might have been had I followed her advice, but I didn't because, after all, Julie knows best! It took me around twenty years to realise that she might have had a point. For someone who loves to take shortcuts, on this particular journey, I definitely went the long way around.

If meditation had genuinely helped me with stress management all of those years ago, I might still be sitting at my desk in the corporate world, capturing business requirements and drawing up process flows. That would have required me to take her advice on faith and that broke two of the programmes that were running in my brain at that time. Firstly, I needed proof, and secondly, I was still living under the great misapprehension that I had to be the smartest person in the room and no one else was going to tell me what was good for me. No, the clever thing to do in this situation was to ignore all advice and spend the next twenty years finding out for myself. Whilst this is amusing in hindsight, I wouldn't like you to think that I set out on a twenty-year mission to understand meditation because I didn't. I filed all of that advice in the 'pick that up later drawer'. This is the drawer where we store all of our hopes, dreams and curiosities. We live in some vain hope that one day life will stop its demands long enough for us to grab a mug of tea, sit on our bedroom carpet and open up this emporium of ideas so that we can begin to carve out the life we really want for ourselves.

It was 2003 when my yoga teacher advised me to meditate just before I left the corporate world to open my coffee shop. With my newfound busyness, I didn't have time for fun or nurture, so I gave up yoga. Maybe if I had stuck with it, I'd still be stretchy and agile rather than hobbling around the house on my knackered heel with my achy lower back. When I attend yoga now and find myself beached in the squashed pigeon position, having a quiet little sulk in the corner of the studio, I long for those days when I could drift in and out of those poses with ease. Strangely enough, meditation seemed to keep knocking on the door, and it wasn't long before David started visiting the coffee shop most evenings after work. David had found Buddhism in later life and shared audio cassette books with me, which I played in the car to and from work. I was captured by this gentle philosophy and the observations about our dominant ego states; the words made so much sense. Simon also visited the coffee shop weekly and was a teacher of meditation and Qigong, the latter being a practice about the movement of universal energy. After a few weeks of chatting to Simon, I started attending his classes, and whilst I seemed to find the meditation relatively straightforward, the chanting always left me giggling awkwardly.

It seemed to tap into a volcano of nervous energy ready to erupt at any moment. One spring evening, just after our meditation, Simon talked us through a practice he wanted us to try. We were asked to partner up and sit face-to-face to each other. We had to answer the question, "Who am I?" I was paired with Simon, and as I sat directly opposite him and heard the conversations firing up around us, I stared into the abyss. I had no idea. I realised I had absolutely nothing, and it brought me to tears. I didn't know who I was. When I'd quit my corporate role, it became startlingly obvious that I'd been playing a part for ten years, but this wasn't who I was. I'd learnt quite quickly that my sense of self had been defined through my career, a career that no longer existed. This wasn't just an internal observation; it impacted how other people perceived me. The corporate world was one of mutual respect but when I worked in the coffee shop, there were people who treated me dismissively and I noticed that some would have attitude bypasses when they realised I was the owner. Suddenly, I would become worthy of their acknowledgement.

This is the trait that can go unseen as we inadvertently align people to the roles they play, imagining their place on an invisible ladder of superiority or inferiority. When we're on the receiving end of such assumptions, it impacts how we interact, and it's described well through transactional analysis. The psychology of transactional analysis is that we all have access to three styles of communication, the parent, the adult and the child. Ideally, we communicate as adults with both parties feeling an equal part of the engagement. However, if someone assumes a position of superiority, they're adopting a parental style of communication that can leave us dropping into our inner child feeling small, defensive and petulant. This parental power play really taps into our rebellious nature but once we're aware of this, we need to overcome our urge to retaliate and respond as an adult, treating them as an equal. This can be a challenge because we'll feel a need to rise up from the position they have assumed for us. Behaving like an adult is our responsibility, whilst their tendency to treat people as inferior based on the role they play in society is their challenge. This attitude might be so deep seated within them that they have no awareness of it. In school, we were taught about the career roles we should aspire to and the jobs that said that we weren't bright, hadn't worked hard enough or hadn't amounted to much. I understand the desire to motivate us to become the best version of ourselves, but this narrative marginalises the non-academic contribution to society that's crucial to how we live. Mindfulness values the interconnectivity of everything. In order for a surgeon to perform an operation, the practicalities are that they eat, sleep and use the loo. They're dependent on an infrastructure of people who pick food, pack vans, deliver food to stores, stock shelves, clean toilets, clean operating theatres, manage, order and create surgical supplies; climb on a motorcycle to deliver blood; the list goes on. It can be really enlightening to pick something you rely on every day and consider all of the activities and the people who made that possible for you. So, getting back to meditation, if you believe in universal answers or serendipity, you might be thinking I'd had three signposts telling me to meditate. What can I say? I guess I just wasn't ready.

I didn't really have time. I was too busy repeating all of the things that weren't really working out for me. When I closed the coffee shop in 2007, I went back to my IT career, where, just for the sheer fun of it, I experienced a couple more episodes of feeling burnt out. It was 2017 when my intuition finally began nudging me in a more permanent direction. I'd developed a close relationship with one of my work colleagues and when the company created a funky new coffee area, we used to meet there for our work meetings. We also spent a considerable amount of time contemplating the pointlessness of our existence and the general meaning of life. We had common interests; Elspeth had a strong yoga practice, and I agreed that I should probably do something about resurrecting my squashed pigeon pose.

During one of our chats and general moans about work, Elspeth recommended a book called *The Miracle Morning*. Well, who doesn't want a miracle that you can order online for only £8 and my mornings were awful. Mostly, they consisted of me making a cup of tea, climbing back into bed and wondering what I could do in the next thirty minutes to get myself out of going to work. The brain loves repetition, and the answer was always *'nothing, just get on with it'*, but that didn't stop me from following this ritual five days per week. Absolutely intrigued for my miracle, I took my little fudge fingers online and this is how I found myself, curled up in my chilly conservatory, a few days later, reading a book at 5am. The book opens with some powerful life-changing stories, which I found completely unrelatable. As stuck as I was, I never dreamed that any sort of change was possible for me. Long gone were the days when I woke up filled with drive and purpose, eager to start the day. I was a working-class woman with a well-paid role. What was there not to love? I was tethered to the treadmill of life, living for the end of the day, living for the weekend, and living for our holidays. I was going through the motions and had completely lost sight of what made me feel alive. I had paper success on the outside and a longing for something different on the inside. Unfortunately, I didn't know what that looked like, so how could I solve it or make a plan? Plus, not finding a career particularly fulfilling didn't feel like a good enough reason to leave.

The first thing I loved about *The Miracle Morning* was life reclamation. As I curled up in that draughty room, for just one hour a day, I felt like I was taking back some of my life. It's a concept that still feels very strange, because who does this life belong to if not to us? How do we travel so far from who we are that we wake up living someone else's life? How did I get here? The book recommends getting up an hour earlier every day and to dedicate that reclaimed time to a set of six practices, spending just ten minutes on each. The chosen practices are based on the author's research into the habits of successful people. One of those activities is meditation, and mine was really simple. I focused my attention on the word calm and simply repeated the word in time with my breath for the entire ten minutes. After following *The Miracle Morning* for a few days, I began to feel sharper, more focused and light-hearted. I generally felt less weighed down by the worries of life. I imagined this was all due to getting up early and feeling on top of my game instead of my usual morning rush.

Every lunchtime, I loved to escape from the office and walk down to the Mersey estuary to take in the views of the river. It was an effort because it's so easy to sit at the desk and work through, obsessing over the busyness of everything. On one particular occasion, just as I was leaving for my walk, I bumped into a colleague from another building. The minute I saw her, I thought *Oh, here we go!* She was a born talker, and I knew that this chance meeting would seriously jeopardise my walk time. Overwhelmed by English politeness and the desire to be seen as kind and understanding, I stood by quietly nodding as she offloaded her current trials and tribulations. It was the usual office stuff, troublesome team members, the lack of direction, the lack of acknowledgement for her efforts - it's truly amazing how much life can be sandwiched into a ten-minute conversation. However, it's what was happening to me that surprised me most. As she was speaking, I could feel all of the energy of the day disappearing. My morning buoyancy was collapsing as my energy shrivelled like a deflated balloon. I could feel myself weighed down by the challenges she was offloading, like I was literally picking up her emotional baggage and taking responsibility for solving all of her problems. Instead of enjoying my walk, I spent the entire time worrying about her, going through the details of her situation and trying to find solutions. I felt exhausted and didn't know how I could face the rest of the day with all of this worry on my mind. But right there, I had a light bulb moment. Yes, my energy was draining, but this was the first time I'd ever been aware of how someone else's emotions were affecting me and it really had me wondering. How often had I taken on other people's emotional baggage or responsibility for their issues? I'd often been described as a moody child, but now I was curious about whether I was allowing myself to get weighed down with other people's problems or at the mercy of their emotions. My colleague's challenges weren't my weight to carry; this was something I could let go of.

I would later learn that this sharpness and awareness skill was born out of meditating for just ten minutes per day, so this is what my yoga teacher might have been trying to tell me fifteen years earlier. The advantages of meditation were not the only gift from *The Miracle Morning*. I became open to other opportunities around me, and I discovered experiences that would never have naturally been on my radar. We think that we can imagine every experience we might ever have, like they're already laid out before us, and we get to choose the ones we want. It's hard to imagine that there's an entire world out there filled with ideas and concepts that are beyond anything we're currently aware of. I liken this to living in the same house for fifteen years, believing we know the property inside out. One year, we decide to redecorate. If you're anything like me, you might already be getting overexcited as you imagine that trip to the DIY store to collect those lovely little sample pots. When we strip back the paper in one of the rooms, we discover a secret door that has been covered over. Fifteen years and we never knew this existed. We're in awe of what might lie beyond as we turn the handle and push the door ajar. Peeping inside, the room is filled to the brim with books, ideas and images that stretch our imagination into territory beyond our wildest dreams, re-igniting our passion for life.

The Miracle Morning is just a book and yet somewhere in its pages, we find our inner self awakening. Tuning into the author's ideas and recommendations, I find myself listening to an online conference hosted by Sounds True. This six-day experience is packed with thought-provoking talks by spiritual authors and teachers from all over the world. It's free, so for the next six days, I tune into as many sessions as I can. Whilst their talks are powerful, I'm most struck by their warmth. There's a gentleness and nurturing in their delivery that's alien to me. It feels like acceptance and safety or like coming home. They describe the weird thoughts and emotions that spin through my life, and I realise that they know human nature; they know me. A few weeks later, I'm searching for something to build on my NLP knowledge and discover a mindfulness master's degree at Oxford. I'm shocked that a subject such as mindfulness warrants academic study and more so that the entry criteria is clinical. I don't have any of the experience they require, but I'm already hooked on the idea and so the search for the next chapter begins.

Inside My Head

Originally, I started this chapter with the usual definition of mindfulness, the one I share in my classes and on retreats. The definition breaks down into three parts and I can reel off the meaning of each quite easily. Yet within the setting of this book, the words seem alien and out of place. Without any context, it's too easy to say, "So what!" or "Who cares?" What we really want to know is what it can do for us. Where can it take us? I've taken you through many of the experiences that have formed my emotional landscape, and there's more to come. In this chapter, I'd like to invite you inside my head. Don't panic, it's a few hours at most. I'd like to say, "Come on in, it's safe and cosy," but there was a time when it was utter chaos. Yes, I'd signed up to a mindfulness programme but much like buying that gym membership, it's the turning up that delivers the actual results.

By the time I found the master's programme at Aberdeen University, I had just two days to submit my application. The fallout of joining late was that the accommodation for the first weekend retreat was all booked up. Well, that's not strictly true; there was dormitory-style accommodation available, but every single part of me knows that shared rooms are not for me. The teaching days ran until 9pm, and I knew I'd want to retire to my room to recharge. I find chatting to strangers a real effort and I was worried that any expectation of making polite conversation would leave me irritable. When it comes to telling people how I feel, I just don't have that tool set and assume it should just be obvious to them. When they don't recognise the signs, I feel justified in my sharp tone, followed by hours of regret and then apologies. I think I need to stop doing it this way. It's not very helpful and doesn't really work. Saving myself from this predicted emotional turmoil, I found a bed and breakfast in the nearby town of Moffat, just twelve miles away. I was very pleased with how I'd solved the accommodation issue; I had a lovely space at the top of a Victorian house overlooking a field of horses. I can nip along the motorway to Chester in around twenty-five minutes, averaging a speed of sixty miles per hour. Moffat was only twelve miles from the monastery, half the distance, so easily doable. I was a problem-solving genius!

I checked myself in on Friday afternoon and then drove across to the monastery for the evening introduction sessions. Driving back around 9pm, I began to wonder whether all miles were made equal. I hadn't really appreciated the challenge of driving in the dark along bendy Scottish B roads, teeming with wildlife. The Saturday classes ran from 7.30am until 8pm with plenty of breaks along the way. It was the breaks that I found the most challenging. Both the teachers and students were absolutely lovely, but sometimes entering the dining hall and choosing the table I'd sit at, took me back to being at school, and it felt like an unspoken popularity test. When I got back to the B&B on Saturday evening, I climbed straight into bed, only to awake on Sunday morning feeling absolutely wiped out.

I stayed in bed a little longer, missing breakfast, but it didn't help. I took out the timetable and began rehearsing the day, imagining how I'd get through each session, feeling as tired as I did now. The guided sessions would be okay, but the breaks would probably be awful. I'd feel under pressure to have light conversations and to make people believe I fitted in, and I didn't have the energy. People would conclude that I was surly or withdrawn and that would be it, no friends for the entire course. This mental rehearsing wasn't just restricted to a day, approaching the weekend, I'd identified the gaps in the program where I'd have an opportunity to disappear on my own to recharge. I'd liken it to the way some of us feel like Monday is a forty-hour day. I saw the weekend as a three-day block, where I would feel out in the open with recharge points along the way. It's odd to observe these thought patterns but at the time, this approach to life was very normal for me.

The more I thought about the day, imagining how I'd endure each session feeling completely exhausted, every instinct was telling me to go home. This is when complete chaos broke out. I can only describe it as two opposing voices in my head rowing with each other. I was learning about mindfulness and the first voice was reminding me to honour how I was feeling and rest. The second voice was telling me to get on with it and push through. I was tired. What was the big deal? The voice of rest came back with a counterargument. *Push through, yes, that's the way forward. After all you've been pushing through for forty years and look where that got you.* I didn't know what to do for the best, but I just couldn't imagine getting through the day feeling this worn out, so I did what any normal person would do, and ran away. As I drove to the petrol station, I realised that I couldn't get in touch with anyone to let them know I was going home. I could find the details at home but that would be too late. To avoid the potential hassle of just disappearing, I wondered if I should just go to the course, more internal arguments! I filled up with petrol for the long trek home and stocked up on a nutritious breakfast of cookies and cake. I headed towards the M6 service station that overlooks a lake, and after a few hours of driving, stopped there for a large bucket of coffee. I still wasn't ready to be around people, so I took the coffee to my car. It was absolutely pouring down as I sat with my hot drink, watching the rain bounce off the windscreen. I felt the warmth of the coffee as I wrapped my hands around it taking in the aroma. I listened and watched as the rain pounded away.

Somewhere in this moment, the thoughts and sensations of the day began to settle down and it felt like absolute bliss. When we describe mindfulness as being in the moment, this is exactly what we mean. Tuning into the sights, sounds, textures and feelings around us and just letting our thoughts come and go. It was ironic that I was escaping a mindfulness course because in this mindful moment, alone in my car, I reset and everything just settled down. I could have easily driven back up the motorway and returned to the rest of the course lectures. What stopped me? More fears about how I would explain myself; I just didn't have the words. As I continued home, I worried about not completing the first weekend and whether this would jeopardise my prospects. I'd failed at the first hurdle. Could I really do this? It was probably a mistake to think that I could pull this off.

Even if they did let me stay and complete the modules, had I forgotten how I'd scraped through two dissertations? Maybe I should just give up now before everyone discovers how out of my depth I am. On and on the mind went, literally pummelling away at my confidence. As a diversion from this inner destruction, I turned on classic FM. A familiar violin tune came on; it was my grade seven nemesis, the tune that had turned me away from the violin forever. It had just been too difficult to learn, but what if I hadn't given up? I didn't see myself as someone who gave up, but what if that was who I was? Once again, the mind was at play, but alongside the internal judgement was a curiosity. I couldn't quite place the name of the musical piece, but in a strange way, it felt apt and relevant. It was a minute or two before the title came to me. It was called meditation. *How funny*, I thought, surely that was a sign that I was in the right place; I was doing the right thing and everything would be okay.

The terms mindfulness and meditation are used interchangeably. It's important to understand the subtleties of each because labels matter. How we label an experience sets our expectations about what that experience actually is, for better or for worse. The founder of the British Mindfulness Association, the late Rob Nairn (1999), describes mindfulness as *'Knowing what is happening, whilst it is happening, without preference.'* When we compare my experience to his definition, it truly reminds me of one of those awful health and safety videos. You know the ones where they do everything wrong to highlight the point.

Staying on site might have been easier, but seven years on, I still don't consider myself dormitory trained. When I woke up on Sunday morning, I was tired and that could have been the end of the story. *'Knowing what is happening, whilst it is happening'*, Nairn (1999) refers to the skill of being with our experience as it is. Feeling tired was my truth at that moment in time, but this wasn't acceptable. Just like the definition states, I preferred to see myself as resilient and energetic. Tiredness merely suggested that I wasn't capable of what lay ahead and certainly didn't align with my perfect sense of self. In an attempt to pacify those fears, my mind worked through the entire timetable and rehearsed every single session to assess whether or not I was up to it, before deciding that I wasn't. Having assumed how I'd feel all day, the mind then went on to predict how I'd behave and how complete strangers would react to me. With the ability to predict the future at that level, I really ought to be buying more lottery tickets. The body never actually left the B&B, and yet the mind had driven over to Samye Ling monastery and rehearsed an entire day. Had I been able to tune into my physical experience, I might have been able to separate what was real and what was constructed in the mind. Instead, this mental rehearsal simply prolonged the sensations of feeling worn out, leading to even more overwhelm and mental exhaustion. The mind's predictions about the day turned out to be false because when I sat in my car and reset, I felt differently and better able to face what was expected.

This is the very nature of our thoughts and emotions. They are temporary and pass through. It is our clinging onto them and running with the storyline that keeps them around longer than is necessary, particularly when those storylines are tied into deeper fears. Whilst part of me wanted to honour my feelings, I was criticising myself for being tired and also for considering that I should just push through because historically this hadn't served me. This internal lose-lose dilemma allowed complete confusion to reign, so going home and returning to a point of safety was literally the 'flight' response in action. Our tendency to judge is fast and powerful. At my fittest, my physical body could run one hundred metres in twenty seconds. I can hear you judging! My judgement fairy can bolt from under her mushroom at the rate of a thousand miles per second. However, not all judgement is obvious to us. What was stopping me from turning up and telling the truth? Oh no! What would people think about that? Could I be getting older or slowing down? This is the battle of non-acceptance of how things actually are, especially when they don't match up to how we want them to be. Judging how I felt simply escalated the fear response, and where did I get those ideas of how other people would behave, with no evidence to back it up? Sadly, those views all come from within because I can only predict the behaviour of others based on how I might think or judge myself in that situation. If I can't honour my feelings, how can I imagine other people honouring them? Even today, did you recognise that I spent the entire paragraph laying down the context so you'd understand why I was so tired? I needed you to believe that my feelings were justified, when it's irrelevant because the body knew I was tired and that was it.

When the mind tells a story, it whips up our emotions, inviting them along for the ride. The power of self-observation is seeing the mind in its true glory and one of the best analogies is to imagine ourselves sitting on the bank of a river. Maybe we notice the ducks and the plants and scowl at the intruders, like the litter or the odd shopping trolley. Our idea of the perfect river probably doesn't contain a shopping trolley, but we acknowledge that it's there whether we like it or not. Our aim is to sit on the riverbank observing without judgement, allowing the river to pass by. We don't have to jump in and meddle with the contents. Mindful awareness is sitting by the river and watching it all, the thoughts, the feelings and the physical sensations. When we're not aware, we've fallen into the river and are swept along by its flow, bumping into the shopping trolley or working hard to avoid it. We're simply reacting to everything that happens to us. Whilst mindfulness describes a way of being present with awareness, meditation relates to how we train. Focused attention training is a powerful way of developing this deep awareness. In the body scan, we practice focusing on a particular part of the body. In other practices, we use our breath as a focal point. People can get frustrated when they first notice their busy minds, but this is how we start. Each time the mind wanders, we bring it back to the focal point without judgement. Initially, we only notice the wandering mind when the meditation guide speaks, but the more we practice, the more we're able to notice this wandering before the guide prompts us. This is how our awareness develops.

We notice we've fallen in and climb back out. We're practising becoming the watcher on the bank, choosing which experiences we interact with. This skill can be used to interrupt our thoughts and destructive emotional cycles, and the more we practice, the quicker we're able to notice that we're caught up in a story. Tuning into our senses, like I did with my coffee, is also a powerful way to bring us back down to earth. These techniques can change how we feel in a given moment. However, there's growing scientific evidence that these practices alter the wiring in our brain, Hanson (2009). In *Altered Traits,* Goleman & Davidson (2017) explain the effects mindfulness and meditation can have on our traits. The brain has billions of neural pathways that behave like an information highway, passing details from different parts of the mind and body. These pathways influence our behaviour, and the interactions we repeat most frequently will be represented by strong neural pathways. The pathways behave like muscles, getting stronger each time we use them.

Through meditation practice, we train our awareness to intercept those patterns that don't serve us, whilst building new, more productive paths. Each time we climb out of the river versus reacting, we're diverting from an existing neural pathway to a new one. Every time we choose the new response, we strengthen this pathway. Mindful awareness is powerful enough to challenge long-term habits and to recognise destructive patterns that take us down the same unhelpful routes. We don't have to dig up and analyse every habit. Our awareness shines a light on where our habits lead so we can let them go in favour of something more positive. We will still fall into the river many times, but we will gradually see the situations that don't work for us. No longer content with dropping or correcting, we are able to identify baggage that we simply don't need to pick up in the first place. The term neuroplasticity refers to our capacity to rewire neural pathways. It's supported in the research of Davidson & Begley (2012), who illustrate how meditation changes the positive and negative connections between the executive part of the brain and our fear response in the amygdala. Their research concludes that we can rewire our neural pathways to make us less susceptible to reactive fear-based emotions.

I've described mindfulness as a skill we learn, but in fact, it's more of an uncovering of something we already know. The thinking part of the brain develops when we're around seven years old, so up to this point, with no ability to predict, we live in the moment emotionally, sensing our way through the world. As the mind develops, we learn to see ourselves through the eyes of others.

Even though this seems like a solid approach, it's all based on interpretation, guesswork and sometimes feedback. We enter into a complex game of mind reading, interpreting the reactions and body language of others to determine how we're perceived. We use this information to create a sense of who they want us to be and correct our behaviour accordingly. This goes beyond people pleasing. It's a combination of fitting in to survive and measuring up to our perfectly created ego. Somewhere along the path, we lose sight of who we really are. The body has no expectations about who we should be, which is why it's a perfect ally in the discovery of our authentic self. Minds are beautiful tools, but as masters, we overestimate their logical capability. They tap into our emotions, recharging them and leaving us at the mercy of this invisible cycle of turmoil. Hawkins (2013) suggests that our emotions are an outward expression of our energy flow. In mindfulness, we're returning to who we were before these powerful minds ran away with themselves. Yet, if mindfulness is within our default setting, why have we lost sight of it? Why is it so difficult to live more mindfully?

The Inner Gremlins

The peak hour traffic was in full force as I turned towards home on my early morning walk. Then, just two hundred yards from the house, I found entrepreneur Steven Bartlett slouched in a large grey cat basket at the side of the dual carriageway. *Wow, how amazing,* I thought. I rushed over and was just on the verge of striking up a conversation when a man in a red sweatshirt turned up on his bike. He stopped, put both feet on the ground and with no invitation whatsoever, started to speak to Steven. I contemplated waiting for him to go, but he showed absolutely no intention of leaving. With an inward sigh, I decided that Steven would probably much rather chat to him than boring old me, but the very least I could do was get a picture to send to my friend Helen. Desperate to share this exciting encounter, I asked, embarrassingly, if I could take a selfie. Unfortunately, my short-sightedness has not improved since reaching fifty, and as I proceeded to selfie mode, I managed to open the photo gallery. My brain froze, and for what felt like forever, I just kept clicking on a photograph of me and two friends, wondering why nothing was happening. How could I make myself look so stupid in front of this impressive entrepreneur and the irritating intruder? Keen to save face, we all pretended that the picture was a complete success, and I set off towards home.

I was a little deflated, but this was short-lived as a few moments later, I went up to my attic room where I found Steven and a small group of friends gathered on and around a double bed. I'd been given a second chance to speak to him. Whilst the others engaged in various questions, I sat on the bed eating a slice of Victoria sponge cake. Even with the impending sugar rush, I couldn't think of a single thing to ask him. So, when the conversations eventually died down, I quietly persuaded one of the other women to take a photograph. I couldn't wait to send it to Helen; she'd be so excited. As I imagined her shock at receiving the image, I felt a little deflated. What had I actually gleaned from his amazing business brain? How could I tell my friends that in the presence of such genius, I'd sat on the bed eating cake? They'd think I was a complete loser. Yet it felt wrong harassing him. How must it feel for him? I wonder if he believes that everyone wants a piece of him. Perhaps sitting on the bed eating cake was a welcome surprise.

Before you stock up on Victoria sponge in the hope of enticing Steven into your attic, I should point out that this was a dream. I've never met Steven Bartlett; I don't think he sleeps in a cat basket at the side of the road, and I have no idea whether or not he likes Victoria sponge. This dream occurred one morning in my snooze window, just before I was fully awake. The night before, I'd watched epigenetics expert, Bruce Lipton, on YouTube explaining how we learn our behaviours in three ways, cognitively, through habit and an early form of hypnosis. The early hypnosis refers to how we download information emotionally ahead of our cognitive reasoning, developing around the age of seven years old. Downloaded information and what we practice form the neural networks that become our operating system.

The pathways are strengthened through repetition, forming habits that often sit outside of our awareness, but are clear to those around us. These patterns unwittingly drive around 90% of our daily interactions. Just before we fall asleep or wake up, our brain wave slows down to theta waves, and in this state, we're able to access our subconscious operating model. So, was this dream an insight into my subconscious beliefs? Does this serious mindfulness teacher prioritise eating cake? Do I believe that Steven would rather speak to other men than me? Do I think that men find me boring? When did I decide that my friends think I'm a loser? This last one is definitely not true, and I'll be interviewing my friends to prove it as soon as I finish this chapter. The point is, we don't see these ideas pulling on our strings like a deranged puppet master.

Mindfulness opens a window to full awareness of our mind and body experience as it arises. Before the development of our busy minds, we only had the option to live in the moment, so what stops us from being mindful and resurrecting this powerful skill? What lurks in the shadows ready to jump out and jeopardise our experience?

When I was hiding out in that Moffat B&B, I had an overwhelming urge to go home. I wanted to feel safe, but what was I escaping from? Putting mileage between myself and the monastery made the decision to opt out of the day simpler and yet everything I was running away from was captured in my mind. It was all travelling down the motorway with me triggering emotional turmoil and draining my energy. We can't outrun our thoughts, and Moffat was the perfect example of a threat that didn't actually exist. When the fear response was triggered by those contradictory thoughts, why didn't the executive part of the brain downgrade the alarm and settle everything down? It might look like the mind was logically assessing the situation to solve the problem, but it wasn't.

Our human safety mechanism is reassured by certainty, which is why thoughts about the unknown easily trigger the fear response. The brain can initiate worrisome thoughts as it appears to search for a solution. The irony is that we take a fictional scenario from the future and bring it into the present, churning up our anxiety and experiencing all of the negative emotions we are trying to avoid. Unfortunately, the more we practice worrying, the better we become. We rarely examine the contents of our thoughts or question their validity. Instead, we react to thoughts with more thoughts. According to optimalhappiness.com 95% of our thoughts are repetitive and 80% are negative. Williams et al (2007) observe how thoughts arise as completely unfamiliar, so we treat them as entirely new and unique. This repetition is down to our brain's tendency to run on automation because this powerful device at the centre of our lives is designed for efficiency. Scientists are discovering that keeping the human body going is thirsty work, and the brain doesn't want to busy itself dealing with the minutiae of our daily existence. It cuts corners, quickly assessing situations to find similar matches before digging out an existing program that looks good enough. This is what we refer to as our automatic pilot.

When we're learning, the brain is fully engaged, which is why novelty or new skills keep the brain in shape. If we're learning to play the piano, we're instructed to place our right thumb on middle C. Initially, it's tedious as the brain digests the information, finding the right key and navigating the thumb in the general direction. After a few attempts, the brain recognises the pattern and creates a little program called 'place your right thumb on middle C'. Now, without even looking at the keys, we can place our thumb on middle C and the other four fingers also fall into place. It isn't long before we can play five or six notes without looking at the keys. No further thought or analysis is required; the brain has a program for this and can climb back into its hammock on a beach in the Caribbean. As the wiring in the brain behaves like a muscle, each time we practice middle C, we strengthen this neural pathway.

Bruce Lipton describes this as learning through habit, but we initially learn through a form of hypnosis that develops its own set of programs that become habits. Aristotle said, *'Give me the child until he is seven, and I will give you the man.'* I was startled by this analogy when I first heard it in my mid-thirties. When we see ourselves as career professionals completely in control of every aspect of our lives, it's a little unnerving to reflect on what will have influenced our early years of development. Much like our evolutionary path where the executive function was a later edition, our early human development relies on us feeling our way through situations. We navigate the first seven years emotionally, building those neural networks in the brain. Millions of automatic programs formed from our interpretations of the emotional interactions with our caregivers, teachers, siblings and even the school lollipop person. Irrespective of the development of our own self-esteem, if we look at two babies, side by side, we wouldn't question that they both have a right to be loved and nurtured. As we instinctively turn towards our immediate caregivers expectantly, there are no guarantees that they're emotionally equipped to provide the safety and comfort a young child requires. If our emotions are shut down, marginalised or met with aggression, we develop programs to contain them to avoid these painful consequences, Davidson & Begley (2012). I'm forever haunted by the phrase, 'If you don't stop crying, I will give you something to cry for.' The veiled threat implies we cry for the sake of it, or that maybe it's the responsibility of others to decide what we're allowed to get upset about. We cannot know what that child's internal world looks like at that moment. A child who can't find nurture at home might perceive the outside world as unsafe. If our emotions are honoured and nurtured, then our programs reflect this.

The analogy glass half empty or full suggests that positivity is a choice, but it's our wiring that makes us prone to negative or positive thought patterns, patterns that drive our emotional landscape and our energy. Surely this is worthy of attention. Yet we live in a culture that trivialises emotions as Davidson & Begley (2012) remind us. Their scientific community advised them that their careers would be detrimentally impacted if they progressed with their research, which can be found in *The Emotional Life of Your Brain*.

Typically, we're programmed to ignore our emotions until they go wrong. Then we're suddenly expected to be able to clearly articulate this complex inner world that we began building as a toddler. But hey, we have those super brains, don't we, the ones that wake up when we're seven years old. Don't we get a chance to revisit our programs when the big brain comes online? Once we have formed our basic understanding of the world, we see the world through a filter that validates our original assumptions. When we're wired to expect hostility or adversity, we notice those experiences. Just like the social media algorithms, our early programs seek out familiar experiences that make sense, even when they're not in our best interest. Each time we affirm our programming, its wiring gets a little more bedded in. When we encounter an alternative, we reframe the experience to align it with our belief structure. So, if we expect adversity and someone is kind to us, we're more likely to treat the experience with suspicion, doubt or mistrust as this matches our pre-conceived ideas of the world. We're at the mercy of these neural pathways that run our lives unchallenged, Sapolsky (2012), Hanson (2009). When I collected my colleague's emotional baggage, I had a subtle sense of her emotional energy. What weighed me down most were the feelings of responsibility, so neatly programmed within my psyche, that I spent thirty minutes trying to solve her issues before I realised what was going on. These early programs critically define how we navigate the world. Yet we never revisit them. This is why Hawkins (2013) suggests that we remain within a few energy levels of our automatic programs unless we learn to transcend them through mindfulness.

As we train our focused attention and learn to notice our experience, something really powerful happens. We're able to tune into what is known as the mindful pause. Between our initial speedy reaction and the automatic program, there's a 15-millisecond pause. Through practice, we can slip into this space, choosing a new path and intercepting the automatic programming. Imagine walking through a field of long grass and taking the path where the grass is worn down. This is the easy route because it's been travelled many times. When we detect a challenge to our safety, we also choose the well-worn path. Whether our fear starts in the mind or the body, what we do next depends on the programming along our path. For better or worse, our pre-programmed thoughts feed the experience, driving our emotional energy. Those thoughts can either prolong the fearful experience or settle everything down. To master our emotional health, the mindful pause gives us an opportunity to choose a new path and each time we do, we strengthen the neural network, leveraging neuroplasticity until the new path becomes our new automatic program. This is why Goleman & Davidson (2017) positively relate mindfulness and meditation to permanently *Altered Traits*. By intercepting the autopilot, we're building a set of programs that serve us better. Mindfulness purists would argue that our destiny is not building new programs but living in the moment with our experience exactly as it is. Living wholly in awareness is not where I am right now and until I am, I'll settle for a better roadmap for navigating *The Emotional Hustle* of life.

When we see our familiar patterns and recognise where they lead us, we have the choice to let go of the ones that no longer serve us. It's this letting go that makes our minds more spacious. We don't create space by suppressing thoughts. We just learn not to engage with each one. In this newfound space, we achieve the clarity to see our inner world more clearly, but it doesn't always live up to the lofty expectations of our ego. The ego wants to keep us safe from hurt so it taps into our natural tendency to avoid seeing those parts of ourselves that don't measure up. It also criticises us and stops us from moving beyond our comfort zone. This style of self-sabotage doesn't create the foundations for growth, but the answer isn't to challenge the ego. We must recognise that the ego's intention is to protect us and to learn to honour its efforts with kindness. This is the work of accepting all of the parts of our humanness, even those that we might not like. Seeing our true nature can be a form of suffering, and Chodron (1994) suggests that compassion arises when we approach our pain with kindness. Self-kindness makes space to see our experience and get closer to our true nature. It creates the conditions that help us to flourish, but this approach can feel alien. When self-kindness feels like a challenge, we may be prone to avoiding it or dismissing it altogether.

Before we write it off, we're reminded how worrisome thoughts can drive negative emotions. This neural method also applies to positive emotions so kindness can strengthen feelings of contentment. Professor Paul Gilbert (2013) believes it's a crucial part of our emotional balance. His model of our emotional state describes three settings, each with a purpose and hormonal impact. The oldest, fastest and strongest is our survival setting, which is designed to keep us alive and is connected to our sympathetic nervous system. It fires up that adrenaline rush when we perceive we're under threat. The second setting is our drive system, which I'd describe as the seeker or problem solver. When the threat system's safety requirements need to be met, for example, we need food or shelter, the drive system solves the problem, thanking itself with a release of the reward hormone, dopamine. The threat and drive settings work well together, which is why we head to the shops to buy shoes or open a bottle of wine when we need comfort after a tough day. We literally reward ourselves to get over a bad day. It's this form of reward that can get addictive, and it's not unusual for these first two parts of our emotional system to become dominant. Sirius, the Greek god, is destined to continually push a rock up a mountain, and when it reaches the top, it rolls back down to the bottom so that he can start all over again. In this single image, I instantly recognised my own striving and achieving.

What happens when we achieve something that we have worked towards? Do we rest in contentment and savour the moment or are we already on the lookout for the next challenge? The third part of Gilbert's emotional model is linked to the parasympathetic nervous system, which leaves us feeling safe and content. It's the rest and digest mode, which is activated by doing something we enjoy, just for the sake of it. When we're in that state of just being, our body releases the contentment hormone, oxytocin, the one that scientists have observed being mirrored between a mother and her newborn baby.

These emotional settings are powered by our neural networks, and their strength is dependent on what we practice. We often need to practice contentment to balance out the powerful and dominant threat and drive system, but it can be a challenge. Often, our culture prioritises hard work and competition over leisure pursuits, and when we feel under threat, it's the leisure pursuits that get dropped. These are the very activities that support self-nurturing. Have you ever been on holiday and instead of enjoying the break you've dreamed of for so long, you spend the time planning your next adventure? Your rock just rolled back downhill. Our contentment setting can be impacted by how we live now but it's also been shaped by how we were nurtured and learnt to nurture ourselves. Sometimes we make space for comfort, but those hours are sabotaged when messages of guilt creep in from our dominant threat and drive systems. There's a nagging sense that if we don't work hard enough, we'll be punished by some unseen force.

Mindfulness brings awareness to that inner dialogue and the habits that are so deeply entwined with the sense of who we are that they feel completely unquestionable. It is difficult to be with uncomfortable experiences because we're hard-wired to avoid them but through kindness practices, we develop the compassion to be with difficult thoughts and emotions. When compassion-based self-acceptance creates space to explore our pain, the body begins to reveal its deepest secrets.

The Voice of the Body

I didn't know Katherine was a psychotherapist or I might have been a little bit wary about talking to her. I always imagine that counsellors and psychotherapists can see inside your soul, like every word, action, and posture is on show, leaking the information that you're not ready to share. Unaware of her mighty powers, I agreed to go to her house to experience Kinesiology and to see if it could uncover the source of my lack of energy. Katherine lives on one of those wide, tree-lined roads in Liverpool. It's not a main A road, but a few roads up where the bird song is louder than the cars. Her house has a Christmas card red door that opens onto a welcoming hallway. There's a parquet floor where her little Westie dog dances eagerly, awaiting attention from someone new. I'd warmed to Katherine's quirky charm immediately when she was a guest on my wellness show. The radio show aired weekly, and I interviewed wellness practitioners in an attempt to dispel the myths that seem to shroud holistic practices. I wanted to give the listeners an insight into what they could expect from different approaches to health.

Kinesiology, also referred to as human kinetics, is the combined study of anatomy, physiology, biomechanics, neuroscience and psychology, Wikipedia (2005). Katherine and I started with the simplest test of all, food allergy checks. It involves bringing the body into contact with a vial that represents a single food matter. The body should stay strong. If it weakens, it's a sign of intolerance. Ever since Slimming World told me that chicken was a fat-burning 'speed' food, it's formed around sixty percent of my diet. This is a tad unfortunate because as the chicken vial came within two feet of my body, I felt my strength drain away as my muscles turned to jelly. It was the weirdest experience ever. Kinesiology supposes that when it comes to our health, the body has all of the answers, and to drive those answers out, we test it by asking questions that have a yes or no answer. The body demonstrates a yes by remaining strong and a no by losing its strength. What followed next was a fascinating decoding method where Katherine asked my body whether my energy issue was physical. It wasn't. She asked if it was psychological, but it wasn't. Finally, my body remained strong when she asked if it was emotional. The questions continued to explore whether the condition was created in the left or right side of the body before identifying the age at which the problem first started.

Using this method, Katherine was able to home in on situations that I'd long forgotten, even though they'd clearly left their emotional legacy. These incidents lived in my body as unprocessed, trapped energy, which Katherine released along the meridian lines, following the principles of Chinese medicine traditions. These ancient practices recognise energy as the life force that flows through the body in the same way as our blood. Nagy (2022) explains how Eastern practitioners came to understand blocked energy as the cause of adverse symptoms. Energy healing practices such as Reiki or Qigong rebalance our energy circulation, improving our metabolic and cellular health.

Western scientific research is beginning to gain a clearer understanding of these traditional practices, concluding that the body does store emotional events, Damasio (2000) and Van der Kolk (2014). Maté (2003) is particularly interested in the invasive nature of our overactive fear response, believing that it feeds stress and potentially contributes to cancers and dementia. There is a great wisdom within these bodies of ours, if we choose to listen.

When we're under the age of seven, we have space to tune into our feelings, there is no mind to interrupt, but as we move through childhood, our bodies become unfamiliar until we reach that age where we need them to be attractive. At school, it's the mind that's exercised all day, and it will be the mind that gets us through all of those tests. Damasio (2000) says that we've forgotten, *'We are not thinking machines that feel; rather, we are feeling machines that think.'* This might be something we have never considered. Even the term mindfulness is misleading, starting as it does with the word 'mind'. The practice of awareness considers our entire experience, our thoughts, emotions and physical sensations. Yet it's the body that gives us a direct knowledge of our experience and tells us how we actually feel. The mind is often laden with cultural expectations or societal conditioning, so it tells us how we should feel, and it gets upset when the body shows signs of not quite living up to those expectations. What happened when I felt tired? Complete chaos, all of which came from the mind.

One of the gentlest approaches to re-familiarising ourselves with that inner experience is the body scan. It's an easing into mindfulness that still serves even the most advanced practitioner, and to this day, I include it on every retreat. When I slow down the pace and guide people to focus on different parts of their body, sometimes they fall asleep. Inspirational teacher and spiritual leader Nhat Hanh (1998) observes how these busy minds of ours, destined to run away with themselves, simply need rest. In his warm, accepting tone, he suggests that if the mind rests for a few minutes, then so be it. Following the voice of the guide, the body scan leads us to tune into the physical sensations in the body, starting with the toes and working our way up. It's not about visualising the parts of the body but reminding ourselves how to sense into what our physical sensations are. It deliberately starts at the feet, to take us as far away from the mind as possible. During the practice, we are training our attention to focus and developing that powerful trait of noticing the wandering mind so we can gently bring it back to our body. When we are able to apply this approach to our everyday life, noticing returns us to awareness. We climb out of the river to observe our experience. Familiarisation with our physical sensations and mental activity is ideal for stress management because once we can tune into the sensations of stress arising, we can take action to balance our breath and reset the nervous system. We achieve this by counting the breath to make the in-breath and the out-breath the same length. It's a powerful approach because the breath is connected to the nervous system, so balancing our breathing wakes up our rest and digest system, making us feel calmer.

As I found out in Moffat, the mind can take any situation and blow it out of proportion. Focusing the mind on breathing and counting disrupts this tendency, so it also calms down the mental activity of stress. One of the great myths of meditation is that people with busy minds can't meditate. The language of the body scan is to observe our experience just the way it is. We return the attention of our busy minds to the focal point many times continually reminded that this is part of our practice. There's nothing to get right. We simply set an intention to be with our experience as best we can. As we notice the sensations in the body, allowing them to be just as they are, we're learning to overcome our tendency to identify them as good or bad, recognising that labels often influence how we react. Approaching whatever comes up with neutrality helps us to challenge our instinctive nature to avoid discomfort or experiences we perceive as negative. Similarly, we can let go of our tendency to cling to joy so tightly that we almost strangle it away. Acceptance takes us closer to letting go of those internal battles that drain so much of our energy. The powerful body scan can also be frustrating if we don't set an intention of just being with what unfolds. When we hold onto the idea that it's supposed to be relaxing, we're left feeling disappointed when the experience doesn't match those expectations. Sometimes the frustrations we experience in the body scan shine a light on our natural tendencies.

We adopt compassion to create a container for our practice. It becomes a safe inner world where all experiences are welcome to come and go, even the difficult ones. The language of the practice is kind because this is the antidote to the inner critic, and it helps us to turn towards uncomfortable experiences without judging them. Coming back to our experience again and again, just as the body scan teaches us, is challenging, as our self-protecting nature will distract us to avoid facing our difficulties. The practice begins to teach the brain that we are safe and slowly we are more able to sit with our discomfort. As we become more of an observer, we can put space between us and our experience as we notice the 'we' who is able to watch those thoughts, feelings and physical sensations passing through. Seeing ourselves in this way suggests that we are bigger than our experience and that neither our emotions, physical sensations, nor even our mind defines who we are. Our inner confidence develops as we build an authentic strength and self-trust. These are the foundations for going deeper because, lurking beneath our anger or hurt, there is usually a story, buried within our subconscious, but powerful enough to drive those destructive emotions we find ourselves drowning in.

Accepting our experiences as they are might seem contradictory to previous chapters that describe how neuroplasticity can rewire the positive and negative connections in the brain, Davidson & Begley (2012). I'm not suggesting that we work hard to replace negative emotions with positive ones. The true role of awareness is to recognise our experience for what it is. The wiring in the brain runs on autopilot, so for better or worse, we are very much at the mercy of those thoughts that drive our emotions and energy. What we observed in Moffat is that our thoughts are often not true.

When we train our attention, we develop a mindful pause that allows us to intercept the automatic pilot before it goes off on its emotional rampage. We're not suppressing what we don't like but learning not to get caught up in false storylines. The wise observer begins to choose how we respond rather than just being subjected to our automatic reactions. With experience, we come to appreciate the natural ebb and flow of our emotions, and we realise that permanent positivity is an unrealistic expectation and can just become another stick with which to beat ourselves. Whilst we can't always fully trust the stories in the mind, being with our experience in the body scan gives us insight into our inner world. Having the strength to be with this world, just as it is, is the foundation of personal transformation. Those irrational reactions that seem disproportionate to our situation are moments of pain that often hold windows into our programming. We can't force those windows open, but when we are ready to accept it, the mind and body bring our programming into the light. Something that's been destructive, but well-hidden is revealed in all of its powerful glory. Seeing deeply into this inner world loosens the grip of these programs. They may still hang around, but we're no longer at their mercy, and each time we see them for what they are, their power weakens a little more. It's a process that the mindfulness community refer to as insight. When I was willing to sit with my experience, my inner programs appeared like fireworks.

The Guesthouse

The famous guesthouse poem is attributed to Rumi and is often linked to acceptance. It can also apply to neutrality and willingness.

This being human is a guest house.
Every morning a new arrival.
A joy, a depression, a meanness, some momentary awareness comes as an unexpected visitor.
Welcome and entertain them all!
Even if they're a crowd of sorrows, who violently sweep your house empty of its furniture,
Still treat each guest honourably.
He may be clearing you out for some new delight.
The dark thought, the shame, the malice, meet them at the door laughing, and invite them in.
Be grateful for whoever comes, because each has been sent as a guide from beyond.

RUMI

Creating Willingness Fireworks

Speke is described as a township on the River Mersey or as a suburb of Liverpool. Teeming with large housing estates and an industrial explosion of factories and car manufacturers, it looks at first glance like a modern phenomenon. Yet, behind this façade lie the remnants of its medieval roots dating back to circa 1066. Later additions to the settlement include the beautifully restored Tudor mansion, Speke Hall, and if, like me, you're partial to a thatched cottage, just 1.5 miles away lies the quaint village of Hale. Just across from the retail park are the original airport and aircraft hangar in all of their art deco glory. The airport car park, now a hotel, is still home to the remnants of old aircraft, and when I began working in the area, I sent photographs to my brother, who, despite having a fear of flying, is a bit of a plane spotter. The airport features in 1960s footage of The Beatles returning home to thousands of adoring fans. Behind these historic buildings are large industrial units. When I worked here in the early 2000s, the estate was non-existent with just a couple of office structures surrounded by fields. Twenty years later, the development expands from the dual carriageway to the sea, but surprisingly, the plots have been carefully curated to sit amongst parklands. The roads are lined with water features, trees and hedgerows providing a haven for small birds and ducks. I'm enchanted by the birdsong that surrounds me as I cross the car park each morning.

Over the course of working in this location, my life has changed dramatically. Initially working as an IT consultant, I began to build a mindfulness coaching business alongside my career. Ironically, once I'd started this journey of self-discovery, it was working in a corporate environment that gave me some powerful insights into my inner landscape. We imagine that our deepest learning can only come from following in the footsteps of monks and pilgrims spending days alone to find ourselves. One of my mindfulness teachers shared his experience of living in a box for many months. I'm guessing that this type of alone time isn't your typical spa break. We need an intention to do the work, so that we can be with our experience as it is. It might be that new adventures accelerate how we face into our inner world, but the truth is, we can start anywhere, even with what seems familiar. The deepest education into ourselves can be had right on our doorstep. *'Wherever you go, there you are.'* Kabat-Zinn (1994).

When we lay the foundations to bring neutrality to our experience, it doesn't make it instantly okay. It's easy to drop our tendency to rise to the bait in situations that bother us a little bit, but what about those that impact us viscerally? When we feel under threat, we retaliate first and regret later, but it's these experiences that really make us feel something, or the situations that plague our minds all day, that provide those powerful insights into our deepest secrets. When our fight, flight or freeze jumps to attention, every single defensive thought we have will be directed at the other person.

It's counterintuitive, but this is the moment to let go of the narrative that directs our attention outwards. It's our willingness to sit with our inner world that reveals the root cause of our issue.

It was the sensations of wanting to retaliate that gave me my first hint that something odd was going on. When one of my work colleagues invited the team to a presentation about his area of expertise, having been in the industry for nearly thirty years, I wasn't expecting anything particularly revolutionary. However, I could find the time to hear him out. He was conscientious and ambitious, and I admired him for that; I certainly had no axe to grind. The team sat in the collaboration area following his presentation on the large digital screen at the end of the table. A few slides in, my internal world was kicking off. He wasn't telling us anything we didn't already know. As he continued, and while I sat nodding politely, I was overcome with an urge to undermine him. I could feel my anger rising alongside the desire to ask an awkward question or throw in a sarcastic comment. I mean, "honestly, did he think that I'd been born yesterday!". If it wasn't for the months I'd spent studying mindfulness-based insight, I've no doubt that a passive-aggressive statement might have flown across the table before I'd had an opportunity to think better of it. This would have been followed by an afternoon of apologising and wondering why I felt the need to behave in this way.

It was so hideous seeing this nasty spark in my personality that part of me just wanted to shut it down, pretending that it hadn't happened. Yet even the petulant child in me recognised that here was an opportunity to put my practice into action. With an insight assignment looming, I was also aware that I had very little to write in it. All of the books I'd been reading talked about deep seeing and how freeing it was. This was definitely a moment of extreme inner awkwardness and cringing. Wouldn't it be just marvellous to turn it into personal growth? At the very least, that mindful pause had given me the space to overcome the urge to make a comment and disrupt the presentation, but I told myself that's not the point of insight.

So, just like I'd learnt on the course, I observed my inner experience without judgement, resisting the mind's urge to overanalyse. I watched the desire to put this person in their place and observed the story lines about my intelligence being insulted. I felt patronised and marginalised. Did he think I didn't know this basic information? Did he just see an older woman who dithered around as an analyst with no concept of how the rest of software delivery worked? (Cue a brief distraction to Bridget Jones, fannying around with the photocopier.) Didn't he know that I'd implemented ACTUAL projects, tested software and trained customers? On and on the stories went, all provocative and threatening to take me down various rabbit holes. I followed the training and kept coming back to the breath again and again. It became an anchor to cling to as I weathered the storm of emotions, grappling with those desires to react. The stories continued to flow, each as triggering as the last.

As I write this down, it appears as though I sat there for hours with the world whirring around me, but it all happened within a few minutes. Then it stopped and as if from nowhere, insight exploded like a firework, with multiple ideas spontaneously occurring at the same time. New stories, new ideas, and new feelings arrived but these were from memories. All at once, I saw the small, brainy child put on a pedestal whilst the parents brimmed with pride, telling anyone who'd listen, how clever I was. My body felt the weight of their expectation that I should always be the smartest child in the room, and it also felt the pain of disappointment when I let them down. Everything was competitive. I remember playing musical chairs, the game where children circle a set of seats and sit down when the music stops. During each round, a chair is removed and the child without a seat leaves the game, whilst the child who gets the final seat wins. When I googled the game to remind myself of what it was called, it was described as a great team icebreaker. I just found it a source of great anxiety. If I lost, Mum would be irritated. I'm convinced it's why I get seat anxiety when I'm queuing to get on a train. My parents would be disappointed when I didn't know something or didn't come first, so I learnt that being clever was the way to gain their affection. My siblings and cousins could see the fake pedestal and enjoyed my toppling or fall from grace. For me, being smart was about being loved and avoiding the hurtful comments of failure. Whilst the presenter went through his slides, my mind and body were tapping into every occasion where I'd perceived parental rejection or been hurt by ridicule. This entire backstory was embedded into the inference that I wasn't intelligent or experienced.

Everything I'd been studying rang true because bringing this out into the open has had a profound impact on how I respond to situations. When I recognise the patterns of the story cropping up, I acknowledge them as the smartest person's story, and it doesn't need to go any further. When the story was deeply embedded and I couldn't see it, as Hawkins (2013) suggests, I was very much at the mercy of that emotional baggage. I recognise the shadows of historic hurt, even now when my family members still comment, "I can't believe you don't know that you're supposed to be the smart one." I realise that this is part of their story and their programming. With an adult lens, I recognise the absurdity of that expectation, the one where I have to know absolutely everything. This invisible responsibility has been an exhausting weight to carry, and it's a relief to put this baggage down. Back in the room, I was pleased with myself. This was going to be a fantastic assignment, and it was because the very next day, the insight fairy paid me another visit. Unfortunately, I felt like I'd taken myself to the brink of a heart attack. Ah, the extremes I will go to, to secure a good mark!

My colleague and I had been leaderless for several weeks, but it wasn't a problem. We were experienced and happy to step up to the extra responsibility whilst recruitment was underway. Everything was running smoothly. So when we were invited to a meeting with the senior management team, we were confident that our efforts were about to be recognised. Unfortunately, our high expectations were squashed almost immediately as our programme lead began questioning what we'd been up to.

It was an odd approach from him, considering that he'd worked with us every day and had full visibility of our efforts, but the line of questioning was purely for the benefit of the senior managers. This is why we were on trial in this harsh, aggressive and poorly executed meeting. Whilst we thought we were going over and above, there was an inference, a contrary view that perhaps we weren't fulfilling our responsibilities effectively. I was absolutely enraged by the theme of the meeting and even sensed that the programme manager was angered by the approach we'd taken, despite him working quite closely with us. I tried to keep my cool until I could escape the office to clear my head but even when I left the building, the events of the meeting circled my mind. I found it impossible to calm down as I replayed the event over and over, completely consumed by my emotions. Leaving the contents of the meeting behind, my thoughts turned to my escape. Another job, another resignation. I didn't want to stay here, but what if I moved to a different company, and it was just the same? It was pointless, I just had to leave work completely and downsize the house to minimise any financial responsibilities. I have come to know this story well. It's my flight story and all roads lead to one problem that my mind has yet to solve. How do I support my lifestyle without an income? Consumed by this familiar problem and weighed down by the emotional turmoil, I didn't recognise this as a story. What I became aware of was my breath getting shorter and shorter. As my throat became tighter and I began to go dizzy, it was the fear of having some sort of heart attack that brought me to my senses.

I decided I ought to sit down and crossed the road to a park area where I found a bench. I was desperate for solitude, to calm everything down, but I wasn't alone. Perched on his tractor across the field was a man cutting the grass, stealing my peace and quiet. I needed to stay seated, so this would have to do. As I brought my attention to the movement of my breath and tuned into the nature around me, a calm, gentle peace started to descend. Watching the breath, I anchored my attention, allowing my thoughts and feelings to come and go. I began to recognise my flight story and the all too familiar problem-solving routine. If I were willing, here was an opportunity to be with this experience and observe the noisy stories. I felt calmer but also frightened of what I might uncover, and in this moment, I felt grateful for the distant company of this human being mowing the grass. The normality of him going about his life was a soothing break from the horror movie running through my mind. We were subtly connected by our mutual presence, sharing this space in nature. As the mist of irritation began to lift, I reflected on the couple of comments that had given me the sensation of feeling under attack. I'd experienced resentment towards the programme manager, but it was my perception of his anger that felt most threatening. Yet the more I searched for evidence of his anger, the harder it was to find. As an empath, it could be something I sensed, but it wasn't outwardly expressed. It began to dawn on me that in reality, irrespective of who had said or done what, I'd brought the anger and aggression into the room. I hadn't expressed or acted on it, but I'd created it within myself. I'd turned a couple of comments into a story.

It's tough to take responsibility for our emotions, particularly when we're wound up into a frenzy, because who would do that to themselves? Targeting that anger at someone else, particularly when blaming them, releases us from our responsibility to do the work. In blame, there's no requirement for us to explore what lurks beneath. When we're willing to consider our part in the exchange, there's an opportunity to face our own challenges. I was devastated to realise that I'd brought all of this anger into my experience, whilst seeming to project it onto someone else. This awful experience had taken me to the brink of a panic attack, and yet it had also delivered a powerful gift. If this anger truly was my own creation, then surely it was within my power to stop bringing it. I had a choice to stop putting myself through this type of harrowing experience. I never had to experience this ever again.

Cultivating the willingness to be with our experience and uncover these powerful insights means overcoming our tendencies to avoid discomfort or grasp at those storylines that validate our experience. When we become defensive, the mind goads us into attack mode, creating excessive emotional and mental noise.

Anchoring our attention to the breath has the power to still this commotion. Through this process, we are able to create the space to explore our experience objectively and to see it more clearly. When we bring our hidden beliefs and automatic reactions out into the open, we stifle their power over us. These movies we play can be unpleasant but until we see them, we live very much at their mercy. When we approach our experience with harsh judgement, there's a danger that we shut down our learning, so we need kindness to turn towards all of our experiences openly. Once we see the seeds of our beliefs and habits, we understand why they were planted and can acknowledge the coping strategies we've developed that lead us down the same path again and again.

This inner knowing is where mindfulness can lead us. What may begin as a calming body scan weaves its way to an improved self-awareness and eventually the knowledge of what lies deep within us. It's a knowledge that can empower us to break free of destructive patterns. There are stories within that are so powerful that, unaware of their spell, they can trap us in turmoil for hours or even days. Once we bring them into the light, we live alongside them, not under them, slowly unpicking their power. Hanson (2014) refers to this as taking the dandelion out by the root.

163 Dandelions

I remember that early spring day, scrolling through social media and seeing a reel of a bumble bee stumbling around. He looked a little drunk and I wondered if he'd overdone his nectar quota or spent his afternoon dozing in a large glass of red wine. The post suggested he'd been poisoned by the gel that we put on the leaves of dandelions, in the faint hope that they'll be taken out and we'll never see them again. I felt guilty and considered whether, for the sake of the bees, I could let the dandelions be. Maybe I could practice acceptance! I swear, as I set that intention, the universe advertised it to every dandelion seed within a fifty-mile radius. A few months later, there were 163 dandelions, taking advantage of my generosity. No ordinary dandelions but little clusters of dandelion families with kids and grandchildren, completely covering the lawn. As much as they danced in the breeze, I couldn't summon up Wordsworth's delight. *Dandelions* and *Daffodils* both begin with 'Da' and are both yellow, so why was he obsessed with daffodils? Had he seen my lawn instead, would we now be killing daffodils and treasuring our daisy-headed dandelions? My dandelions did look like daisies and who doesn't love pretty white daisies covering the lawn with summer snow? So, what is it about the dandelion that we struggle to accept?

I tracked down an article in Science and Nature to find out more about this prolific little flower. According to Welti (2020), the dandelion was valued for its medicinal properties and was exported all over the world. It even appears in the lineup of other botanical beauties in Claude De France's *Book of Flower Studies*, published around 1510. When nectar is in short supply in early spring, it's the humble dandelion that feeds the bees and the butterflies, whilst some species of birds are known to feast on dandelion seeds. So why do we stare upon this hero with such disdain? How has it fallen so far from grace? Welti's (2020) article suggests that the dandelion has become a victim of the human obsession with status.

Owning land allowed us to grow our own food, but it is also synonymous with wealth and accomplishment. As our habits changed and we stopped working the land, owning land for the sake of owning it boosted our outward appearance of success. This was epitomised by the neatly manicured lawn. As humans cooed over their little green squares of toil and pride, the dandelion became the symbol of the lazy gardener. To the birds, bees and butterflies, the dandelion is everything, yet it truly is a victim of time, perception and culture. We struggle to accept its place within the natural order of things as we wrestle for perfection removing anything that threatens this pursuit. Our cultural backstory tells us that the dandelion is the intruder. Yet this idea is alien to the creatures dependent on it. It's our lack of acceptance that continues to threaten its existence.

I believe this humble flower can show us both sides of the coin. We, too, have our bees and butterflies, those people who truly see us and naturally lift us up. We also have our non-accepters who have us jumping through virtual hoops justifying our choices. Their interest isn't motivated by their desire to get to know us. Instead, it requires us to validate our way of doing life.

There's an inference that we're not quite following the normal path, and it's our responsibility to align or explain! We can be treasured or vilified depending on the company we keep. Just like the dandelion, how we're perceived is very much the responsibility of those doing the perceiving. It's their backstory, not ours. The value of the dandelion is not lost on the bees, and regardless of our perception, its resilience shines through. It's a reminder that our authentic value also comes from within. Our inner resilience can empower us to transcend external expectations and let go of seeking validation. It's a process that begins with compassion-based self-acceptance, but it can be complicated.

The simple process of accepting a flower in our garden unveils the complexity and origin of those invisible standards we set. It's even trickier when we try to accept experiences that have been emotionally difficult or even traumatic. Perhaps somewhere within our understanding, acceptance has become synonymous with okay. I would never agree that losing my mum so young was okay. What I can do is acknowledge that it happened because that is undeniable. Acknowledgement seems to carve a steadier path through our experience, loosening the denial that can leave us fighting against reality. It alters the emotional dynamics of our experience, and maybe the strand of denial becomes a lesser pain to bear. We can apply the notion of acceptance to the behaviour of others, and this can grow through our ability to recognise the Karmic nature of our experiences. Whilst Karma is often interpreted as a punishment, sometimes it's an invitation to be on the receiving end of our own behaviour. When we've hurt another, even unintentionally, seeing it from the other side can provide a window into our human flaws. Accepting our own infallibilities takes us closer to understanding the complexities of human nature, even those of our junior school bully.

You may remember the pre-social media world when we could leave school safely in the knowledge that we'd never have to see our childhood bullies ever again. Of course, we have choice over our social media use, and we don't need to mooch around in those groups that have an awkward way of leading to something unpleasant. But it's like that obsession with tracking down the new partner of an ex-husband, only to find out that she's a gladiator supermodel. It's a scab we can't help picking, even though that wise little watcher within knows it'll end in tears. Why don't we listen?

In my social media stalking, I came across a school reunion group and was surprised to see myself mentioned in the chat. There she was, my primary school bully, calling out her concern for something that had happened to me when I was nine years old. "Wasn't it awful?" she said, worried that it might have scarred me for life. Did her alleged concern leave me with a warm feeling inside? It didn't! It simply brought back all of those hurtful emotions that arose when it felt like the entire school was talking about me and laughing at me.

It started with the fire drill and lining up outside in the playground. We were playing around and my friend lifted up my skirt, so of course I did the same to her. The teacher was irritated by our misbehaviour, and along with the people who had dared to speak during the fire drill, we were hauled in front of the class for questioning. We stood in a semi-circle in front of the blackboard as he began his interrogation, working around the group, tapping people under the chin to force their head back, or shaking them until he got the answer he wanted. We all stood waiting our turn as the rest of the class looked on. Absolutely terrified, he got just one person away before I wet myself, a small puddle forming at my feet for the entire class to see. I guess on a positive note, the rest of the circle escaped as he awkwardly whisked me off to the receptionist's office. It was my school bully, my alleged friend, who couldn't wait to spread the word, and to her credit, it seemed that by lunchtime, the entire school knew and were coming up to me to ask about it.

So here Amy was again. I'd have loved to have taken her recent concern on face value, but she'd messaged me a few weeks earlier to confirm who I was. I replied politely, asking her how she was, curious to see if there was just one ounce of recognition. There was no personal reply, just this little comment in the school group chat. I wondered how deep her concern ran. How good was her memory? What she'd done to me was far worse than spreading gossip around the school. Within seconds of seeing her comments in the group chat, my stalking led me to Amy's profile, where I was horrified to learn that she was a social worker. Unless she'd had some form of personality bypass, how could she be entrusted with vulnerable individuals? I considered meeting up with her, imagining I could scrape together some sort of closure, but I was overcome with the smallness she'd inflicted on me all of those years ago. That inner fear that bullies tap into still lurks even into adulthood. There had been no physical abuse, just those debilitating feelings of insignificance and irrelevance. We nearly had a fight once, but the showdown was interrupted by a lovely girl in my class. She hung around after school and offered to walk home with me. Along the way, she talked me out of it. I often wonder how a girl of that age has the wisdom or foresight to talk someone out of something stupid, without damaging their ego. She didn't make me feel defensive but appreciative that she had taken the time to be kind.

Initially, Amy and I were best friends, but when the daughter of a football team player joined the class, everything changed. That's when two became three and I seemed to be included for pure entertainment value. I didn't understand what was happening.

I wanted to fit in but also knew that being around them didn't make me feel so good. Despite us having very little money, Mum would go into debt to buy significant presents for birthdays and Christmas. On my 10th birthday, she bought me a beautiful silver signet ring. It was so pretty on my little hands that I just loved gazing down at it. It wasn't long before Amy spotted the other girls making a fuss of the ring and came over to admire it. She made all of the right noises, but I could sense her, like a shark under the water, waiting for an opportunity to attack. When I found myself alone in the toilets the next day, she appeared with her new friend.

They were smiling and sidled over to me as I washed my hands. Even though they pretended to be my friends, my gut instinct was fear, but our class was just across the corridor, so I couldn't imagine them doing anything too obvious. They asked to see the ring and I hesitated, thinking they might try to steal it from me, but they just began criticising it. They called it a cheap fake. After all, how could someone like my mum afford a proper ring? Their words stung, stripping all of the joy from this gift. I felt like they'd driven a stake through my heart, knowing how much my Mum had sacrificed to buy it. I tried to escape and get back to the class, but they blocked my exit. I needed to get away to make the pain of their words stop. It was the love behind the gift that should have been important to me; this was its true value, but they even sabotaged that. "Why would someone like you get a real silver ring?" they laughed. Just as I thought their taunting was complete, they came up with a plan to test it. They told me that if the ring really was silver, I could stand on it and it wouldn't bend. This would prove it was real. I knew it was a trick, and they were backing me into a corner. I was so torn because part of me wanted to prove them wrong and wipe those snidey little smiles from their faces, but I knew it was so disrespectful to this precious gift. I was betraying my mum and everything our relationship stood for. I didn't know what to do to make it stop, so I gave in. The girls smiled at each other as I slid the ring down my finger and placed it on the ground. In a matter of seconds, the beautiful ring that had brought me so much joy lay crushed on the floor. Pleased with their work, they sauntered off to class. I could feel the tears welling up and stinging my eyes as I stared down at the crushed jewellery. How could I ever explain this to my mum, knowing that I'd hurt her feelings so deeply? I couldn't face her seeing me for the shallow, ungrateful, fearful person that I was. When she found the ring on the top of my wardrobe a few weeks later, I told her I'd stood on it by accident. I don't know whether I was trying to protect her feelings or mine, but it seemed the easiest way out and so much more straightforward than telling the truth. Maybe I missed an opportunity to expose my bullies because it wasn't long before they struck again.

I didn't know I was an introvert until I was in my mid-forties and took a test. I wasn't happy with the answer and ran the test a few times, trying to nudge it in a different direction. It made no difference; the jury was out. I was an introvert. As I read the profile of my 'alleged' introvert archetype, lots of stuff just fell into place. Feelings and behaviours that I'd imagined were defects all seemed to be part of the characteristics of the little wizard character right there on the screen. It explained my general discomfort in crowds and my preference for alone time when I needed to recharge but it also reminded me of my fear of group celebrations. This was learnt behaviour and always took me back to the anxiety of my classmate's leaving party. It was held about three miles away from school at a cricket club on a dark country road. Much to my surprise, Amy had offered to give me a lift. It was only accessible by car, so without the lift, I probably wouldn't have gone. I'd bought a small gift but unfortunately left it at home. As the girl who left two violins on a bus, it's ironic that I blame my memory on the menopause!

I could pass the gift on in school, so it wasn't a big deal, but Amy told me that it was totally unacceptable to arrive at a party without a gift. In actual fact, she didn't believe the gift really existed, after all, how could my family afford such things? When we arrived at the party, Amy told me to wait by the door as she went off to speak to someone, and that's pretty much how I spent the entire evening. Sitting on the outskirts, not quite sure how to approach people or make conversation. Being on the receiving end of Amy's comments left me fearing rejection from other children, so in some ways, being on my own felt a lot safer. The hours dragged by as I sat alone in the corner, but I also did a lot of observing and thinking during that time. I didn't want to be left without any friends, but

Amy and co. weren't true friends. I was beginning to come to terms with the reality that my best option was to stay out of their way. I made myself a promise that once they dropped me off at home that evening, our relationship was over. It was a relief when the party was finally finished, and it was time to go home. Amy came back, and we made our way outside. As we stood on that remote, dark country road, waiting for the parents, Amy asked me how I was getting home. Wow! What a bombshell! "I thought you were giving me a lift," I answered. "Oh no, only here," she said. "We only agreed to give you a lift here. I haven't asked my mum if it's okay to give you a lift home. She'll be annoyed if I ask her now!"

Ten years old, in the middle of nowhere, and they were about to abandon me unless I could persuade her mum to take me home. I was so angry and sick of them putting me down and making me feel small. My pride got the better of me, and I told them my mum was picking me up, so it didn't matter. My story was completely unbelievable. We didn't even have a car, so I said she was coming on her bike. They were thrilled by another chance to ridicule me, but I had to start clawing back control. Being on the end of their abuse was beginning to make me feel physically sick. When her mum turned up, she couldn't understand why I refused to get in the car. Sensing something was going on, she separated us and insisted on waiting with me, but I knew that wouldn't work. I protested and another mum stepped in and offered to wait with me. It turned out that she didn't believe my story either, but once

I was seated safely in her van, with the promise of a lift home, I was able to tell her what had happened. To this day, I'm forever thankful for her intervention. She didn't make a great deal of the situation, but it turned out that the girls gave me a wide berth from then on. Shortly after, I learnt to play the recorder and music became my solace. The musicians were kind and fun, and I'd finally found a place where I belonged.

So, this was Amy, growing up to be a social worker. Was it possible that she had a caring nature, lurking beneath? I wasn't so sure. The closest I ever got to care work was working as a cleaner in a psychiatric hospital. As a nineteen-year-old student, I applied for a summer job and found a vacancy at St. Catherine's Hospital. It was an old Victorian red brick building, mostly a home for elderly people who couldn't look after themselves or psychiatric patients.

They were well cared for, but it was a shock to see the demise of human beings, particularly within the surroundings of this dark and grim ancient building with its high ceilings and long, dimly lit corridors. Some wards were locked and as I approached, I'd hear patients crying out. It scared me. Over time, I got to know a little more about the patients and nurses who created these internal communities. They weren't all bedridden, and I have memories of two ladies in their nineties who were relatively able. For me, their presence on the ward was a bit of a mystery.

Elizabeth was what you might call a wily old girl. She was very slim with brown curly hair and eyes that seemed to peer into your soul. The first day on her ward, she met me with a smile and an open box of Maltesers. I politely declined, after all, I could go to the shop for anything I wanted, but they couldn't. It was a lucky choice because it turned out that Elizabeth had an obsession with crafting objects out of poo and her particular talent was Maltesers. She also smeared it all over the toilet walls, and as a domestic, it was my job to clean it all up. The other active lady was called Grace. She had a gentle soul and had been born blind. Both women had been in St. Catherine's since their early twenties or from about 1917 until the current year, 1987. Originally, the building had been a workhouse, and Elizabeth had been incarcerated for getting pregnant out of wedlock. Grace was there because her parents couldn't cope with her disabilities. When the workhouse became a hospital, its doors were no longer locked, but where would they go? What would become of these two women who had no experience of life? Two lives stolen because they didn't fit in with the rules or expectations of what was deemed 'normal' society.

Hospital life was an education. As the youngest in the group, I was a little intimidated by these down-to-earth, worldly women I worked with. One in particular stood out for her confidence, humour and complete disregard for what anyone else thought. She commanded the room with her wit, and I was both scared and in awe of her. When she moved onto pastures new, eager to fit in, I just seemed to take on her persona, becoming outwardly outgoing, funny and most of all the centre of attention. I'd go to any lengths to uphold this comedy character. When a quiet and subdued mature student joined the team, I got on with her pretty well, but elevating myself at her expense seemed to come naturally. She was different, slow and methodical. The other women with years of experience of running their own homes whizzed through the cleaning routines, whilst her pace was a little slower and inexperienced. Whilst the other women might criticise her speed behind her back, I was the one who took it upon myself to say things to her, all in the name of comedy, of course. It was only when I left the role that word got back to me that I'd bullied her. I'd never seen it that way. Yet looking back, I had. This was a habit. If I worked on a team where someone didn't pull their weight, I had a gift of uniting the team against this common annoyance. I was always ready to use humour to undermine someone for the good of the group.

Whilst others would moan and tut quietly, I would be the one to attempt to sort it out, but not in the most effective way, often relying on meaningless banter that didn't really address anything. Sometimes it was driven by my need to take responsibility for other people's issues. Other times, I used it to bolster my need to stand out. For years, this habit sat firmly in one of my blind spots but now I see it for what it is, and I can choose not to rise to those urges. Sometimes my programming still leaps into action, but I no longer need to act on it.

It's useful to consider the difference between banter and bullying, where is the line? I think it lies with our intention. Do we use it to include, build relationships and rapport or is our banter a veiled attempt to ridicule or make a point? We also need to recognise how our banter is received. If our comments make someone feel worse, irrespective of our intention, then we're moving into the realms of bullying. I've wandered into this territory, but I don't want to be the Amy in the room. Amy and I had different motivations for our behaviour but we both marginalised another human being for our own ends.

I've heard that when we forgive, we do it for ourselves to let go of the heavy burden we carry. Those repetitive thoughts and negative feelings can keep us tied to destructive stories, prolonging sensations of fear. We can expend so much energy replaying experiences that have long gone, imagining the outcomes had things taken a different course. Resentment is like swallowing poison and expecting the other person to die, St Augustine (circa 400 AD). Yet, forgiveness doesn't resonate with me personally. There's a danger that it comes from the moral high ground of the righteous forgiving the sinners. Perhaps I don't understand the concept, but what I am able to understand is our human flaws, and through this, these negative experiences become more palatable. I've observed traits in myself that do not serve me well and have harmed others, even though I'm someone who would rather receive pain than see another endure it. Under the right circumstances, the bullied becomes the bully because we're all capable of these human traits. Taking all of the emotional complexity of life into consideration, it's possible to concede, without needing to know the answer, that there was a particular set of circumstances that motivated Amy to bully me. Just like me, Amy was gripped by her own story and her own needs to stand out or survive. Whether she ever recognises it has to be her own work, but on reflection and in light of my own story, what I need to develop for Amy is compassion.

Accepting what I'm capable of as a human being naturally opens up a space to accept Amy's behaviour at that time. It wasn't okay, and we shouldn't marginalise our experience, particularly in light of its profound impact, but as we truly see our human nature, our experience gains more context. In recognising our flaws, we are more open to the flaws of others. This is the path of recognising the human condition and the traits and behaviours we share. Under the right circumstances, I became Amy, but my behaviour doesn't define who I am, just like Amy is not defined by her behaviour.

Perhaps like me, Amy has moments of regret. Perhaps like me, Amy is completely human and prone to destructive behaviour. Maybe Amy is a very good social worker indeed.

What a lot of insight from a dandelion. Now I get to choose whether I accept nature's abundance of 163 dandelions or weed the lawn and empty nature's fridge. As I continue scrolling through the history of the dandelion, I'm drawn to a picture that closely resembles those in the garden. *Here it is.* I smile to myself. *Here's my special little variety.* As I glance down the page, it becomes clear that these aren't dandelions after all, they're Catsears, but that's okay! We love cats, but then there it is in black and white, those unacceptable two words 'false dandelions'. "Well, I never," I retort to myself. "I didn't agree to these imposters, only the real ones!" So, the story of non-acceptance begins all over again. Different players and different themes, but non-acceptance all the same.

Helplessness: The Comeback Tour

Sometimes the only way we can take back our control is to walk away. As we learn to recognise those emotional energies that pull us down and we engage with the knowledge that moves us forward on the journey of personal development, life can feel a little lighter. But it's not always plain sailing. Our habits are tricky and even the good ones can be held against us. I was now a mindfulness teacher with a few years of experience and a strong daily practice. I'd seen some of my inner lurkings and was working with them. Factually, that is where I was, but my mind had developed an entirely different story weighted down with new expectations. I should now be some sort of invincible superhero, ready to withstand the harshest of emotional battles, completely unscathed. As with any expectation, what comes next is our inner berating when we don't quite live up to the impossible dream. Funnily enough, I know this story, and how it all works but sometimes we simply have to experience it, to fully digest the learning.

I've mentioned that I have a side hustle in IT consultancy to pay the bills. What's become clearer is that it's also a great place to learn. I've been talking about writing a book since 2015, and I always joke about those people who will be getting their own chapter. We sit on the mat to train our minds, but it's real life that reveals those hidden gems of our programming. When we bump into others and observe ourselves in difficult interactions, we get to see what lies beneath, if we care to take a look.

So here I am again, in a different role and a different company, and I want to leave. I'm not sitting in the car park crying into my ice cream or having a panic attack, but I'm still worried that I might actually have some sort of work-related allergy. My serious expectation flaw is ramping up the issue by telling me that my skills should be helping me to rise above whatever it is that is making me feel so completely awful. It's a mystery because the role is interesting and I've already made some great breakthroughs. In fact, within a few months of joining, I paired with another third party on some consultancy work, saving the company in the region of £100,000. Usually, when I find something interesting and rewarding, I'm highly motivated and work tirelessly. This is definitely how I started, but something had switched and left me feeling edgy, apprehensive and dreading the day. My rational brain was telling me that there was nothing of significance to worry about, but I felt it. I was drained and literally dragging myself into the office every day. It was starting to impact my mindfulness business. I just couldn't work out what it was, but I knew I had the skills to get to the bottom of it, if I persevered. I had a suspicion that things began to take root during the Christmas raffle. Phyllis was my supplier engagement manager and could be a lot of fun to be around, so it seemed natural that she'd take on the responsibility for organising the Christmas activities. When it comes to raffles, I'm more of a donor than a winner, but despite the draw being laced with booby prizes, to my delight, I did win a decent prize. Unfortunately, before I'd had an opportunity to collect it, Phyllis had decided that I wouldn't want it, and it disappeared.

It was absolutely bizarre but when I mentioned it to my colleague, he thought it odd that it bothered me, so I let it go. Maybe Phyllis gave my prize to him and it's taking pride of place on his desk at home – who can say! I'd like to say I moved on, but the incident lingered in my mind like an unsolved puzzle. It wasn't long into my contract before I was allocated to one of the company's highest-profile projects. It was complex and high risk, so the managing director wanted me to get closer to it. With no programme manager available, I was asked to chair the third-party supplier meetings and ensure everything was documented and tracked. We were just getting into our rhythm when, a few meetings in, Phyllis hijacked the session completely, to chair her own agenda. Because she was the supplier engagement manager, it was a tricky situation to navigate. The very next day after a particularly productive all-day workshop on the project, Phyllis rang me to question why I was spending so much effort on this high-profile initiative. She queried whether this really was the best use of my time. I felt like the rug had been pulled from beneath me. I was doing well and making good progress. I'd also been assigned to the project by the managing director, and Phyllis had witnessed the conversation. Addressing her concerns, I took a step back but asked her to provide clarity on my area of focus. This never came.

As a business analyst, my role involves solving business problems by analysing processes, discussing current issues, exploring ideas for change and then working with technical people to agree on how to move forward. This ability to capture a business problem and facilitate its solution establishes trust with the business representatives. This trust is fundamental to the success of the role and the credibility of the analyst. The business analyst has to decide on the best way to contribute to a project, which might be organising workshops, demonstrations, side by sides or interviews. There isn't a one-size-fits-all approach, which is why autonomy in the role is necessary.

Left with no specific area of focus agreed, Phyllis assigned me random pieces of work. What might be urgent on Monday was already superseded on Tuesday. Despite Phyllis having a different role and skill set from mine, she had specific ideas about how things should be done and how long they would take. Phyllis saw herself as an all-rounder who needed someone who could pick up the detail that would take up too much of her time, but she hadn't engaged an assistant; she'd contracted an experienced business analyst with over twenty-five years' experience. As Phyllis stepped into the key projects, she'd select the meetings to invite me to. Instead of providing the usual continuity and building up business knowledge, I was dipping in and out when a diagram was required or there were details to write up. By then, the relationships with key people had been forged and issues or ideas had been discussed, but nothing had been written down. When I asked the questions that had already been answered, the teams became frustrated at the notion of repeating themselves. For me, this was a challenging way to build good business relationships but that was the ebb and flow. Phyllis was driving the bus and building the relationships whilst I was a passenger, always playing catch-up. Every time I felt I was making headway, I'd be moved to something else.

This was the nature of the culture, as Phyllis reminded me during those many sessions that I organised in a bid to gain some clarity. She had no choice; things had to be done quickly, and this was her motivation for involving herself in every project. I've worked in small, fast-paced companies, so the concept of a quick turnaround or multitasking isn't alien. This was different. It was unproductive chaos.

I was quickly realising that I couldn't thrive in this environment, and I could feel myself withdrawing and shutting down. Personal growth has taught me that survival isn't an option anymore. I want to feel good about what I do. I had an opportunity to leave at the end of my contract but needed to take responsibility and attempt to sort things out. Despite appearances, I had a good relationship with Phyllis, so this was a possibility. Usually, when I get to the leaving stage, I'm so emotional and worried about holding everything together that I cannot find the strength to tackle the issues. I knew I'd made progress as I sat across from Phyllis calmly explaining how the current working practices prevented me from offering the company the best of my skills and experience. I explained that for me personally, the approach was disempowering. Ironically, identifying the feeling of disempowerment was a turning point and very much aligned with a Headspace (2024) article, which pinpointed the lack of control over our workload as a source of stress. I've always linked the emotions of irritation and frustration to stress and have only recently observed how being controlled and manipulated taps into the sensations of helplessness and hopelessness. These emotions are connected to apathy, one of the lowest forms of energy. This is why we have to dig extremely deeply to uncover the strength we need to crawl back out of the hole.

I remained objective whilst I delivered my points, but was met with a childlike narrative. The clarity I needed was absent. Whilst I understood it was impossible to define the work in this fast-paced organisation, defining the expectations from a role that she'd personally engaged, ought to have been more straightforward. Clarity may feel challenging, but it forces us to be honest about what we need and expect. Without it, we're shoehorning someone into a role that doesn't fit or, worse still, employing an expert and telling them how to do their job. During our meetings, Phyllis demonstrated a lack of accountability, blaming the culture or deferring difficult questions up the management chain, where they inevitably became lost in the general chaos. Phyllis was happy to adopt a prescriptive approach to project work but didn't want the accountability that surely must accompany that level of control. When control exists without accountability, it becomes control for its own sake. Management requires responsibility, whereas empty control leans more towards status. Dyer (2024) suggests that being told what to do can be bad for the human soul. Yet when we're in the presence of great leadership or wisdom, we're happy to be shown the way. Perhaps the wisest resist the telling and controlling in favour of encouragement to see the best within ourselves. These are the leaders we admire for their craft and naturally want to mimic their behaviours. Meanwhile, Phyllis just seemed to be playing a game.

When she hinted that I needed to come into the office on the day I was hosting a mindfulness event, I simply didn't rise to the bait. I came to know her hiding behind vagueness as a tactic, particularly as Phyllis could be very specific and direct when she needed to be. She waxed lyrical about the knowledge I could bring to the table, overlooking the fact that I'd been messed around for weeks, whilst she and the team had been working on this project that allegedly so desperately needed my knowledge. Just thirty minutes later, in front of the senior management team, she directly asked me to come into the office for the meeting. It was unnecessary; it was clear from the conversation that other alleged experts were dialling in from home. I stated my reasons for not wanting to attend in person, but they were challenged, so I didn't agree one way or another. As I travelled home that evening and got stuck in traffic for two hours, I knew that being in the office ahead of an important mindfulness event was too risky. Separately, I approached the meeting host, and we agreed I could dial in from home. The week of the meeting, Phyllis rang me. As other people were working from home, she saw no reason for me to come into the office, particularly in light of my event. What looked like kindness was just another demonstration of control, as absolutely nothing had changed since the initial request to attend in person. She was merely giving me permission to do something; I was already intending to do. At the end of this generous offer, she asked me for a favour!

The unpredictable behaviour and the manipulation created an unnerving uncertainty. I simply didn't know what I'd be walking into from one day to the next. The environment was frustrating, but initially it had felt okay, so I was still keen to find the root cause of my underlying debilitation. When our mind and body aren't aligned, confusion reigns, but I know from experience that it's our emotions that provide our personal insights, so this is where I started. I'd tracked my emotions through disempowerment, hopelessness, helplessness and apathy. I knew they represented the core experience because I recalled shutting down and withdrawing when Phyllis first hijacked that meeting. Withdrawal allows us to step back and disconnect, but when it becomes routine, we start to play it small. We give up, to protect ourselves from the confusion that reigns when someone is nice to us one minute and underhanded the next. The same mind fog arises when someone constantly changes their mind with no awareness of this

U-turn and no recognition of its impact. Conflicting behavioural patterns can be so subtle that we begin to doubt our own sanity. Much like narcissistic gaslighting, we are left wondering if we are exaggerating or imagining the entire thing. Once we lose trust in our own opinions, our self-confidence comes under attack. I've seen all of the texts that advise me that no one can make us feel anything we don't want to, but that observation ignores one important fact. Sometimes we're primed to react to particular experiences. Yes, those lurking early childhood programs strike again. As I began to unpack Phyllis's behaviour in the emotional terms of disempowerment, hopelessness and apathy, I realised I was tapping into a very painful experience. Unwittingly, Phyllis's controlling behaviour was taking me back to my brother's 4th birthday.

It was a beautiful spring day in 1973. The birthday boy was smugly fitted out in his new cowboy suit, complete with a waistcoat, pretend gun and cowboy hat. We were playing outside of the house under the kitchen window, fascinated by a piece of plywood covering the kitchen grid. We were taking it in turns to jump up and down on the wood whilst we watched the water from the tap splashing around. For exactly seven days, we'd both be the same age, and then I'd be five. As my brother bounced on the plywood, his suit became snagged on a nail sticking out of the brickwork, and as he moved away, he tore his new suit. At first, he was upset that he'd ruined his cowboy suit, but as I watched on, I saw the colour drain from his cheeks as he was overcome with dread. In that moment, time stood still. The cowboy suit was a gift from our uncle who was staying in our house. We instantly knew there'd be consequences.

We quickly hatched a plan to hide the suit, and whilst Mum was busy in the kitchen, we crept into the house and hid it at the back of my brother's wardrobe. The incident had sucked all of the joy from the day as we counted down the hours in anticipation of our uncle's return home. We were overly good, invisible even, and maybe it was this behaviour that tipped him off. It wasn't long before he asked why my brother wasn't wearing his suit. It was like he could smell blood in the water. There was no amount of playing it down or changing the subject that could distract him. He told my brother to fetch the suit, and I stood in the living room as my brother sullenly walked upstairs to retrieve it. Mum was in the kitchen sorting our tea, whilst my uncle sat calmly at the table, lighting his Woodbine cigarette with a Zippo lighter. The radio played a happy song in the background, and I remember thinking that it was strange that such a tune could be the backdrop to what was unfolding. The world continued to turn, irrespective of our pain.

My panic began to rise as my brother came back into the room with his suit. My uncle invited him to sit down on a chair next to the table. He wet his fingers and used them to extinguish the end of his cigarette before placing it into the ashtray. He started to examine the suit and noticed the tear. He put it down and then casually turned off the radio. Now there was only the huge weight of silence. Across the table was a 1970s tape recorder. It had buttons like piano keys—the red one on the end was used for recording. My uncle checked the label on a cassette tape before placing it into the machine. Intending to record the conversation, he pressed the 'play' and 'record' buttons down together and then began the interview. For what seemed like forever, he asked the same question over and over again. "Why did you do it?" My brother answered truthfully. "It was an accident." But this answer wasn't acceptable, and he was accused of lying. Again, the question came. "Why did you do it?" I tried to intervene and to back him up, but I was shut down, told to keep out of it. On and on, the same pattern was repeated. I knew it would only end in violence. As long as my brother told the truth, the torturous interview continued. My uncle wanted him to say he'd done it on purpose, and once he did, my uncle would be happy. This was the version of my brother he saw, naughty, defiant and out to get him. Best of all, the admission would give my uncle the perfect excuse to punish him.

A belt to his bare backside or sent to bed without food. I was consumed with a deathly dread knowing there was no happy ending: so frightened for him and yet completely powerless to help. As I stood with tears streaming down my face, I felt the familiar warm sensation of wee running down my leg. It turned out it was the perfect distraction. Now I was getting shouted at and told that I was disgusting. I was sent to the bathroom, and my brother was sent to bed without food. I thought for a moment that it was over, but one day, when I returned from school, my brother had been taken away. We moved house, and I was told that I wasn't allowed to mention him. I was confused because he hadn't died, but getting upset or missing him just seemed to bother the adults around me. Sometimes we went to visit him, but it was horrible leaving him behind. I wanted him to be happy, but I was jealous when he made new friends, because he was my first ever best friend. I cried myself to sleep every night. Eventually, sometime later, my little buddy came home, as defiant and wilful as ever.

The energy of reason is powerful when we recognise that our emotional reactions go much deeper than the situation in front of us. My emotional response to Phyllis's behaviour was being compounded by the depths of this historic helplessness. Our reactions aren't always rational, particularly when they're plagued by a history that hides in our blind spot, van der Kolk (2015). Whilst this didn't excuse her behaviour, it did explain why my feelings were disproportionate to the situation and why I struggled to just hold my ground. Phyllis wasn't responsible for that. I could also acknowledge that some of Phyllis's behaviour might easily be part of her own blind spot. What patterns and habits had she adopted to make her own way in the world? What was the backstory that had drawn her to this particular style of behaviour? She might be aware of her desire to control people or outcomes, but in her world, this may seem completely normal. The emotional transaction that occurs between two people can go much deeper than we imagine. Seeing the cause of my own pain was truly transformational and gave me a greater understanding of the energy dynamics between myself and Phyllis. I could let go of my own pain and open my mind to the challenges that she might be facing, understanding how they seeped into my world. I tried to truly see her and, in doing so, felt less engaged with the negative feelings, more able to extend some compassion. I felt less defensive and softer in my approach.

However, it was still clear to me from our many conversations that without accountability for her part in the issues, there was no opportunity to improve our working practices. Being undermined at every turn compromises our psychological safety and our protection is to fight or to disengage. We can shut down and accept our fate as under the control of another, drowning in hopelessness, or we can expend our energy continually challenging the behaviour that is intent on marginalising us. Hawkins (2013) suggests that only our will can overcome this sense of hopelessness and describes apathy as an aggression against the self. Recognising that I cannot change someone else's behaviour, I realised I'd have to fight to cling onto my motivation whilst someone worked in opposition to strip it away.

This wasn't an environment in which I could truly thrive as this would require me to go head-to-head with her style of management. At best, I could survive if I fought to stay on an equal footing or at worst, I'd be constantly dragging myself up from the depths of apathy, shutting down to simply get through the day.

After escaping narcissistic control, I promised myself that I no longer had to put up with this sort of behaviour. I had encountered a personality type that literally weighed me down, thriving as it did on control and superiority. I could have stayed and stood my ground, but I wasn't convinced that fighting to merely survive was the best investment for my energy. Some can contextualise and focus on a greater purpose, and I've known people who've stayed in destructive environments in the knowledge that redundancy might be just around the corner, but we must weigh up the personal costs. How much of ourselves are we prepared to lose whilst we wait in limbo, fighting to survive? Do the financial benefits outweigh the challenges of continually swimming upstream?

So here I was overcoming the need to run away but it was clear that the personal cost of staying was too high. Sometimes we stay because we assume that everywhere is the same or that we don't deserve anything different. Yet every human being deserves to thrive and live their best life. I decided to leave so I could honour my commitment to work in an environment where I could thrive. I was saying yes to me. I knew there was better out there, because I'd seen it.

The Love, Peace and Joy Tribe

The best gift we can offer ourselves is inner peace because when we peel back all of those layers, that's what we all want. It's disguised in the stories of the Caribbean beach, the house without the mortgage and the lottery win. It's the choice to spend our days exactly as we please, feeling safe and content and answerable to no one.

When I watch my seven-year-old grandson playing and using his imagination, I notice how energetic, happy and uninhibited he is. There are invisible boundaries that keep him safe and protected, and every now and then, he bumps into them only to be corrected by the adults. He begins to sense the rules and sometimes looks to his parents first, reading for a reaction before he does something that might not be allowed. Just like our cat George, it's his curiosity that's most likely to get him into bother. Our childhood curious behaviour is how we learn. Yet without doing anything wrong, it can push the boundaries that exist for our safety at that point in time. One minute we're exploring the great adventure of life, the next we've suddenly broken the invisible rules. How does it feel to be corrected? Is it possible to separate the behaviour from that developing sense of who we are? Do we have the context of the adults' decisions, or do these early opinions and corrections become embedded into who we think we are, good or bad? We know in our hearts that newborn babies deserve the best of everything life has to offer. Yet somewhere along the way, we lose sight of our own human equality and our sense of worth becomes diminished.

Growing up, we need to understand the rules of operation. We need a manual but everyone we meet has a slightly different version, so we learn to work out the rules that will keep us on an even keel. Those rules define how we might act, but they do not define who we are. A computer has a manual to explain how it's programmed, but that physical box can be wiped clean and reconfigured with a new set of programs. Just like that PC, we can run Word, Excel or Paint, but we are more than those applications. There's a whole authentic you inside, trying to get out and let's be honest, being authentic is so on trend right now. (She winks!) Our authenticity gets buried behind the stories in the mind and the programs we run on autopilot. Years spent people pleasing or trying to fit in can leave us struggling to identify the very basics of what we need, like how to define our perfect day. The pathway back to our energetic life is through the rediscovery of who we really are. It's our emotions that provide all of the clues, but the mind behaves like a bouncer on the door of discovery, always blocking our way or sending us somewhere else.

When we sit down to meditate, we see this mind bouncing around and wandering off. It tells us that meditation isn't for us; we can't do it and then the judgement creeps in. This bit isn't your personal story; it's everyone's. Yet there are people out there who can meditate, so that tells us that it's possible. The body scan brings us closer to our inner world and other forms of meditation teach us to settle our mind, but inner peace is not a game of whack-a-mole for our thoughts.

We do not learn to squash our thoughts but to allow them to come and go, like seeing ourselves as the vast sky with our thoughts passing through like clouds. When we learn to watch those thoughts, we may see them come into the mind and then drift off. Sometimes I catch something just before it leaves and try and grab it to pull it back in because some of our thoughts are juicy. This is why working with them becomes a skill, and thoughts have babies! Once we cling onto one thought, it leads to another and another until that single thought has suddenly generated an entire family of its own. We step out of the thought party, only to notice we've been trapped, so we re-anchor and begin again. That's the way the wandering mind works. It's not like we see it putting on its coat and trotting off down the street. It wanders off, and at some point, we notice and bring it back.

We are teaching ourselves to sit on that riverbank, observing those thoughts that so powerfully drive our emotional energy. Thoughts that drift back to the past or worry about the future but are so rarely right here with the body. What we see in meditation merely represents what is happening in our world. We can have, what we interpret as, good or bad meditations, because just when we think we've got the hang of it, we experience a practice that leaves us feeling like a complete novice. There's no such thing as a bad meditation because every practice is about becoming familiar with our experience. Meditation becomes a window into life as we practice tuning in to our thoughts, sensations and emotions until life itself becomes our practice. As our awareness grows, we do see those parts of ourselves that don't quite live up to our expectations. We notice how we judge and compare but these are just different stories. Everyone else seems to be doing life better, or getting it right, but it's an illusion because we're all battling our emotional roller coaster every single day. This is the life of being a human being. Our imperfections are those of the human condition. The dandelion grows regardless of how it's perceived by those around it, and we, too, can break away from our dependency on external validation. When we wake up feeling like that dandelion in the middle of the pristine lawn, we need to recognise that often the harsh retribution comes from our own internal judgement. It's digging deep to develop an inner resilience that allows us to be at peace with ourselves, to accept ourselves and to love ourselves for who we are. Whether you think it's corny or cringy, self-love is the foundation of personal growth.

Without the capacity to love ourselves, we hit a brick wall, because it's too difficult to face the extreme standards we set ourselves when we can't meet our expectations with compassion. Sometimes we fear the inner narcissist will flex its muscles and we'll get out of hand, only to be rejected by the rest of the world. Narcissists struggle because they can't find self-acceptance and love. This is why they become so dependent on the validation of others. Gilbert's model is the perfect example of the balance we need. Whilst our dopamine-based reward system delivers happiness, it's often conditional on achieving or acquiring something in the future. It's joy that truly fires up the contentment we need to counterbalance the threat and drive systems and soothe our emotional landscape.

When we first fall in love, joy captures this magical experience. It's like living in colour when we've only ever known black and white. We drift through each day, basking in the feelings of being seen by another. Nothing is too much trouble as we seamlessly float through the challenges of the day. We don't pick up problems but allow them to pass by because we don't want a single thing on earth to upset this euphoria that we are experiencing. This is the invincible joy that we can nurture for ourselves through acts of kindness or compassion. We can follow guided practices that naturally bring the rest and digest system online, releasing the contentment hormone, oxytocin. It leaves us feeling safe, accepted and content. Simply doing something we love also releases the hormone of unconditional love.

Maybe it's just me, but do you find yourself putting off the things you love because you don't have time? Seeing a friend for lunch or a walk, taking up that musical instrument, learning to dance, thousands of dreams sitting on our collective shelves until that new life comes along, you know, the one we actually signed up for. Then, eventually, we wake up at the age of fifty like we've arrived in someone else's life. When we're unhappy in our chosen careers, happiness is reserved for retirement because this is where the magic will happen. At long last, we will have the time to be happy all of the time and not just on weekends. When all of this knowledge was at the forefront of my mind and I sat at my desk for months, writing my master's dissertation, the first thing I was going to do when I finished was to learn to play the piano. Instead, I started a business and a book. I had new things that stole my time, keeping me away from this precious hobby. We become so good at getting by that we don't make time for joy because we think it can wait until all of those other priorities have been taken care of. Whatever it takes, joy must join that priority list because until it does, we're never going to get around to it. Sometimes joy is already here because we're making time for the good stuff, but when our minds are still caught up in that negative narrative, we never truly appreciate what we're experiencing. Have you ever been in awe of a beautiful sunset and then watched it get snatched away as we tune into the fear-based sensations of lack? Our mind gets wrapped up in wanting to hold on to it, wishing all days could be like this one.

In the clinging and worrying we lose the moment. We disengage from this beautiful sunset, which is right in front of us, waiting to be experienced. There's no blame here, because this is our wiring. Hanson (2009) explains how we prioritise safety, negativity sticks like Velcro, whilst positive experiences slip away like Teflon. This is why gratitude practices are popular because we are teaching ourselves to recognise the happiness and joy that is already here. In *Hardwiring Happiness: The New Brain Science of Contentment, Calm, and Confidence,* Hanson (2014) writes that tuning into these little moments and embracing them gives the brain an opportunity to develop and strengthen these happiness skills. Happiness doesn't need to be dependent on us reaching a particular state. We have everything we need right here in this moment.

Our experiences can take us through every level of the emotional landscape from shame right through to joy and peace, but it isn't a linear journey. We don't begin at shame and crawl up the ladder to receive our certificate for reaching inner peace and joy.

The very nature of our emotional energy is that it still moves between these different states. Awareness helps us to develop choice, and at any one time, we are following one of three paths. The first is the path of no awareness, where our stories come and go, and we're very much at their mercy. With some awareness, we follow path two, recognising stories and choosing whether or not we want to engage. On path three, we notice that our experience is challenging, but we can't quite work out why our emotions are being hijacked. Subject to having the skills or finding the right support, observing these experiences can uncover those hidden programs. As we unpack these experiences, they start to lose their hold over us. In time, they become our path two stories because we're able to recognise them as stories and choose how we interact with them. Path three stories often find us, and they're a tough gig. Sometimes we can't be with our experience or move through it at that point in time, but a guided RAIN practice can support us through working with difficult challenges. It's a practice that begins by settling our nervous system and grounding us. We then turn towards our situation to see if we can recognise it for what it is, and accept that it's here with us. The practice moves on through a reflection on the thoughts, sensations and emotions that accompany our challenge before we end by considering whether it's permanent or just passing through.

If you're thinking of skipping the kindness and the joy, I see you. When I first started to learn about mindfulness, I felt like I was hanging by a thread. I was working full time, studying for a master's degree and supporting my elderly relatives. My auntie was suffering from the later stages of dementia, and my uncle was caring for her around the clock. There were ongoing battles with the hospitals and the care process. We'd reach a point of some stability, and then my auntie would deteriorate. We'd find ourselves standing in a corridor for hours waiting to receive care, whilst my auntie lay on a trolley, with no idea where she was. Then, she'd be nil by mouth for several days as we waited for someone to come and assess whether she could swallow. Some days her statistics were so low that she was given hours to live. We'd sleep in chairs to be with her through the night. The staff were always lovely, but the system they operated within was inadequate and ruthless. For six months, my seventy-four-year-old uncle watched on as his partner of forty years faded away, his own suffering pushed to one side. He was angry, and it made me anxious and prone to retaliation. Time and time again, my mindfulness teacher told me that the kindness practice was the answer. It felt like taking a fire extinguisher to a large bonfire. All of the books told me to keep going through the motions, practice, practice, practice, but as I followed the guidance, all I felt was resistance. I needed something to get me through the pain and the exhaustion, so it became my mantra. Driving to the hospital, the nursing home or the house. "May we be happy, may we be healthy, may we be safe and may we live with ease." At the very least, I guess it became a different form of focused attention training and calmed everything down.

I took it on faith and the research of Choden & Regan-Addis (2017) or Gilbert (2013), but I never felt much evidence of its impact. The first time I taught this practice, eighteen months on, I felt the words sticking in my throat. Just like the principle of kinesiology, it was like my body knew I was a non-believer. I can tell you that with perseverance, something beautiful happened, and it really is worth making the effort. Before that reveal, I want to talk about rice.

Emoto (2004) is one of the early researchers trying to show how our thoughts and inner dialogue impact us at a cellular level. He's played music to water and even used three jars of rice to demonstrate his research. The rice experiment became popular and was followed all over Japan. I was so fascinated with the idea that I thought I'd give it a try, and you can find the results on my YouTube channel, *The Emotional Hustle*.

The experiment involves speaking to two jars of rice, daily, over the course of around two or three months. The first is spoken to kindly, and the second negatively. There's a third jar of rice that's ignored. Knowing what I do about energy, I picked the positive jar and decorated it with a picture of Hayley Mills in her 1960s role in *Pollyanna*. This was one of Mum's favourite films and is about a young girl bringing cheer to her local town through her sunny disposition. My husband, Mike, spoke aggressively to the second jar because I certainly didn't want that negativity in my life. The third jar was put away in a cupboard with the loo rolls. My initial expectation was that the experiment would fail completely, or it would follow the expected path and the jar we spoke to negatively would deteriorate. The experiment went as expected, with one surprising outcome. The rice in *Pollyanna's* jar was white and fluffy, with very little separation between the water and the boiled rice. In the abused jar, the rice turned yellow and black. The water in this jar became murky as it began to separate from the rice. The greatest surprise was that the ignored jar fared just as badly as the one that was under attack. It also separated from its water and became discoloured, suggesting that the absence of attention and positivity can be just as detrimental as abusive language. Emoto (2004) has conducted numerous experiments that research the impact of words, thoughts and music on water. This is because humans are made of trillions of cells, and each one is about seventy percent water. Since his work, epigenetics expert Bruce Lipton has also discovered that cell stems develop depending on the environment they are in. For our cells, that environment is created through our thoughts and emotional energy. So, if you're thinking that the mere absence of criticism is enough or that it can be as effective as being kind to yourself, it won't.

'We need four hugs a day for survival. We need eight hugs a day for maintenance. We need twelve hugs a day for growth.' Virginia Satir, as quoted in Forbes magazine (2020)

Whilst that inner love and resilience are fundamental to our personal growth, we are not designed to live in isolation, and who we interact with can have a powerful influence on our emotional energy. Tuning into how we feel makes us more aware of the cultural environments that drive a fear-based narrative and leave us feeling on edge or draining our newfound buoyancy. Quite often, when we're tired or we've had a long day, it can be the entertainment we seek so innocently that strips our joy. Sometimes, we want to be entertained or need a pick-me-up, but some of the media we're exposed to always runs a fear-based narrative. Stories that leave us feeling on edge literally tap into our survival instincts and just don't deliver the restorative energy boost we seek. Seeing the perfect lives on social media might leave us feeling content, but when we're at a low ebb, they can tap into our feelings of lack.

Joy and happiness are at the top of the emotional energy scale, and humour also boosts our emotional energy. No matter how much banter and joviality there is in a relationship, we also need psychological safety. When we sense that someone doesn't have our back or our best interests at heart, we'll still feel guarded in their company. We don't need their validation, but we do need to trust that they'll respect our feelings and our boundaries. Sensing into a relationship helps us to understand if it's working for us. Sometimes the issues are a temporary blip that we know are passing through; other times, we're in an unhelpful relationship that's not going to change anytime soon. It may be something that we want to recover or nurture but we may not be sure either way. It's helpful to consider if it's worth it. Is the juice of the lemon worth the squeeze? Olyphant (2004). Maybe we feel safe in the relationship but recognise those people who naturally thwart our efforts or dampen our spirits. We may be able to survive these connections, but is that what we want for ourselves? Do we stay stuck in the same place because we believe that there's nothing better out there? This belief that everything will be as it's always been becomes our own prison. It also primes our mind to seek out those experiences that prove our point. Just like the dandelion, we can sit on the lawn waiting for our poison, or we can move to the wild meadow to be treasured by the birds and bees.

At the time I left my consultancy role, it was extremely lucrative, which made the decision harder, but I had to consider the overall emotional cost, particularly in light of needing high energy levels, to support my business. It took me a long time to realise that I deserved better, but in a way, I was lucky, because I'd seen better and knew what that looked like. The corporate world of tech in the 1990s was all briefcases, suits and predominantly men. I'd worked on teams that were functional. People got the job done, worked in silence and didn't spend much time really getting to know each other. I noticed a significant change when I moved from a technical department to a retail one dominated by women. Covid had changed the workplace, and we were at home on Microsoft Teams. Most of the calls started with idle chatter, which I found completely alien. Don't get me wrong, it could be a lot of fun hearing about the antics of Freddy's weekend in the hot tub or the best way to keep an air fryer clean, but I wasn't used to it. The team leader had a genuine interest in getting to know who people were. Somewhere during the discussions about data attributes and *Married at First Sight,* strong team bonds were created. For me, there was also something so much deeper. When it comes to the word healing, it's a word I feel viscerally. It makes me recoil like I'm about to admit to an inner failing or weakness. It feels like it's connected to a deep vulnerability or fear of exposure. Yet, this is the only word strong enough to honour the experience I had with this team. When I visited the kinesiologist in Liverpool, one of the trapped emotions that was impacting my energy was the pain of my redundancy. It wasn't on my radar, but I remember being saddened by the lack of acknowledgement from the people I worked with.

It was like I didn't exist. After working with them for eight years, I could only conclude that they didn't really like me, and I must be a bit of a witch. Part of me knew that the team hadn't done anything out of malice, but that didn't make it any less hurtful.

I'd been working with the retail team for around eighteen months and on this particular morning had swapped some hours about so I could teach an online mindfulness class. It had been a frustrating call because one of the students had tapped on his keyboard all the way through my guided meditation. My many attempts to message him to go on silent had gone unnoticed. When I'd finished, I realised I had a missed call from the retail team senior manager and the minute I heard her voice, I knew there was something wrong. The project we'd be working on was getting postponed. The upshot was that I was being given two weeks' notice. Initially, it was a shock, but I also recognised that whilst I was contracting, some people were losing their jobs. Contractors are temporary, so the concept of redundancy doesn't really exist, but this was irrelevant to the team. They were losing a friend and colleague, and they made that matter. For those last days, I literally felt cocooned by the warmth of this team. I didn't want a fuss, but they rallied around, organising the leaving meal that I didn't have the heart to arrange. I felt seen and acknowledged as they showered me with warm wishes, cards and gifts. I wasn't looking for praise or adoration, I guess I finally had validation that I wasn't such an ogre after all.

On a sunny August evening, we sat around the dinner table in a lovely private room overlooking the Liverpool Albert Dock. We laughed so much that I physically ached. As I took in the atmosphere and the company of these gorgeous women and one man! I no longer felt ignored and forgotten. I felt like I'd found my tribe. This is how I came to know 'better', because I found better. Finding my tribe showed me that relationships could be different. When you feel good and you feel seen, nothing less is good enough.

Mindfulness has not been as lucrative as a corporate career in IT, but when it comes to the people I meet through my retreats, it's been priceless. Teaching my book retreats, I have bonded with another group of beautiful women, customers I would now consider friends. The retreat started with nerves, apprehension and a lack of self-belief, but my gut instinct told me that this was something I wanted to do. Often, what we teach becomes the very thing we need ourselves. It was during one of the kindness practices that, for the first time ever, I felt something profound.

I often follow our lunch with a guided practice for compassion or kindness, and on this occasion was guiding the kindness mantra. The lovely book group were in the room, and the leader from the retail team was there too. It had been a beautiful day in their company. As they settled under their blankets, I took my seat and went through the usual steps of balancing the breath and settling the mind before moving onto the mantra. When I guide the mantra, I ask the followers to tune into the sensations that arise as they experience the words. Every experience is unique, but on this occasion, what surprised me was my own. When I first taught the practice, I felt like an imposter as the words stuck in my throat.

On this occasion, as the words entered the room, I felt like I was sitting in a giant bowl of love, me and these women sharing this experience. It was profound and something I would never forget. Kindness works, and scientists have the research from FMRI scanners that illustrates that it strengthens the pathways linked to empathy and joy, Davidson & Begley (2014). Kindness may not be something we can take to easily, but practice works even on us non-believers.

When we recognise that happiness lies in the contentment of being with ourselves or our moments, we realise that we've been looking for it in all the wrong places. All the rushing around and striving fades into insignificance as we acknowledge that the work is to accept ourselves as we are. It's not about changing to match a perfect set of circumstances but learning to be okay with how things are and to let go of those experiences that no longer serve us. This letting go naturally delivers peace of mind, and this is the foundation of joy. It is the stories and the programs that keep our peace at bay, but seeing them for what they are and choosing what we engage with naturally clears the space in our mind. This is the space for inner peace. It doesn't mean we should settle. Acknowledging the miracle of the human being means we owe it to ourselves not just to survive, but to thrive. Being human right here, right now, is a miracle all of its own.

Let's Talk Miracles

Let's talk miracles! Too soon? Oh yes, here we go, I can almost feel those eyes rolling. It's always the same with these sorts of books, isn't it? We read all of the normal stuff and then just as we're feeling relaxed with the author, safe that we're on the same metaphorical page of life, we realise that they're bat-shit crazy.

In her book, *Why Has Nobody Ever Told Me This?* author and psychotherapist Dr Julie Smith refers to the startling statistic that the chances of you being born right now are around 1 in 400 billion. Did anyone else think of a few family members and breathe a sigh of relief? The number gives me a headache. There simply aren't enough characters in my visual space to imagine it. Dyer (2024) observed that nature delivers the human. Then somehow, we forget with a sort of 'we'll take it from here!' attitude. If the creation of the world were down to human beings, it would be delayed and over budget. Can you imagine how long that planning application would take? There's so much truth in Dyer's words. We have become separate from nature, our life source. Yet we feel it, don't we? If we want an immediate energy boost, we book a holiday in the sun by the ocean. We walk up mountains in awe of their vastness. We listen to the songs of the birds and watch in fascination as the blackbird goes worm hunting in the rain, its bright yellow beak prominent in contrast to its dark feathers. These are the rewards of just being at peace in nature. These are the rewards of plugging ourselves into our source.

I know in my heart that the meaning of life goes far beyond my logical interpretation, so I'm open to picking up any clues along the way. It's an inner battle between faith and proof, but it hasn't always been this way. There was a time when I didn't care too much whether the answers came from science or tradition, as long as I had them. I felt reassured that somewhere there was a grownup who knew exactly what was going on. One minute I was content to be a child, the next I felt like I was spinning out of control because I didn't know the rules. From that moment on, it seemed that my entire existence was dependent on understanding the bigger plan. My favourite childhood question was: *'If God created the world, who created God?'* I would gaze up into the eyes of my primary school teacher, the fountain of all such knowledge and wisdom, and wait for my answer with patience, hope and anticipation. Sadly, it didn't seem to matter which way I phrased my question, the response was always the same. She would look down at me, roll her eyes to the ceiling, let out a huge sigh and say, "It's playtime now, Julie. Off you go outside." It was so dismissive that the only conclusion I could draw was that the answer was so obvious that my teacher couldn't be bothered making the time to tell me. It felt like we'd already covered it in reception class, and

I just hadn't been paying attention. Perhaps she'd told everyone else when I went off to change the newspaper in the rabbit's cage. That made sense because my friends seemed totally uninterested too, so I imagined they already had the answer. This mad story morphed into a blind spot belief, one of those lurkers that I woke up to.

For decades, I had this ridiculous notion that when it came to the meaning of the universe, everyone else knew the answer. Others didn't just have the answers. There was a special club of 'knowers' that I was just too stupid to join. I didn't like feeling stupid, so I stopped asking questions and started hanging around on the outskirts of the clever club in the hope that someone might drop a few hints. Eventually, I did what everyone else was doing: I gave up thinking about it and got on with my life.

The challenge with opening our hearts and minds to potential human experiences is that we've been primed. We don't need to logically grasp a concept, but if it's written or spoken by someone we trust, then we are happy to take it on faith. The source of that knowledge matters. Did it come from Western science or from an Eastern faith tradition? Some of us have only known and understood the approaches of human science and feel comfortable with this concept that was formalised clinically around 150 years ago. It seems more tangible than the holistic traditions that have passed from generation to generation for millions of years.

We love proof. It makes us feel safe. Someone presents a hypothesis, they explain how they'll prove it, and then if a set of circumstances consistently delivers an outcome, it's proven. Repeatable results strengthen the percentage of proof, but context is everything. Of six million women surveyed, ninety percent found that chocolate cake enhanced their mood. Of six women surveyed, ninety percent found that banana bread helped them to lose weight. Both of these statements, which are, by the way, completely fictional, show a success rate of 90% but the second study only actually applied to six women. Supposing the first study was carried out by Cadbury? Is there a small chance that they've looked for the evidence that provides the best result? Could M&S lemon cake have exactly the same effect? The difficulty with any research is that to prove an outcome, the test conditions have to be consistent and human beings aren't. There are thousands of variables that impact our interaction with the world. Whether we were the first born or youngest, where we grew up, what our parents were like, where we were educated, whether we liked our primary school teacher, whether our friends were nice, what age our parents divorced, whether we experienced grief, when we experienced grief, and the list goes on. Putting people into a statistical category and measuring the impact scientifically is tough. I'm not criticising science. I'm just saying that the results aren't always as fixed as we perceive them to be. When it comes to treating humans, the easiest way to drive consistent results is to reduce the variables. This is why medicine tends to home in on the specifics of one condition. Once we start considering all of the factors that may or may not impact our human health, the variables start to ramp up, and the predicted results become less guaranteed.

What did we do before? What preceded science? I believe it was a combination of faith, holistic practices and wisdom traditions. For millions of years, we survived this way.

Scientific and holistic traditions both have something to offer. They are not mutually exclusive. When something is proven in science, it means we've found a repeatable pattern. It doesn't mean that practices unexplained by science aren't effective. It just means we don't have the evidence yet.

In the online *World History Encyclopaedia,* an article by Mark (2014) describes the discovery of the oldest love poem, *The Love Song for Shu-Sin,* written circa 2000 BC. I must admit, I was relieved to find it, as, according to my understanding of the latest science, love was only discovered in the late twentieth century. We might even have the Dalai Lama to thank. We know that the emotional studies of Davidson & Begley (2012) were frowned upon by the scientific community of the 1980s, but their book also shows it was their intention to study problematic emotions. The Dalai Lama agreed that he'd encourage his network of monks to take part if the research also explored happiness, contentment and empathy. He'd observed that Western research focused on what makes us ill but never considered what keeps us well. The progress of emotional research wasn't just hampered by our attitude; we didn't have the technology to objectively observe emotions.

We can study physiology by examining dead bodies, but emotional research requires living volunteers. Taking off the top of someone's head whilst they're still alive is frowned upon in polite society, even when it contributes to scientific advancement. Research became much more insightful with the invention of the functional magnetic resonance imaging (FMRI) scanner in the early 1990s. This provided an opportunity to study the brain in action. However, linking love to the hormone oxytocin was irrelevant to us mere mortals who've been experiencing love for millions of years. If there's anything that illustrates how science is sometimes behind the curve, it's love. We've come to see science as the leading-edge vehicle for invention, bringing something new into the world. However, often its role is to discover or explain the miracles that nature already holds. Being clear on the difference between invention and discovery allows us to honour the true gift of nature. The use of electricity was revolutionised by the invention of the light bulb, but electricity itself was discovered. The microwave is an invented box that blasts our tomato soup to smithereens within a few minutes, but it harnesses electromagnetic radiation waves that have been hovering around in the ether, waiting to be found by humans. Are there other miracles hanging around just waiting to be uncovered?

Imagine trying to explain Wi-Fi fifty years ago. Interacting with a loved one, thousands of miles away, via a screen connected through this invisible force. We take this technology for granted but it would have been perceived as miraculous. Is it imaginable that in fifty years we might even acknowledge the human form of Wi-Fi? When I was attuned to practice Reiki, one of the options I began offering was distance energy healing. It's not as futuristic as it first appears. We already understand that facial expressions and body language influence communication as much as our words, but is there something more? Have you ever been thinking about someone just before they ring or text you?

Have you ever walked into a room and sensed the mood? Maybe you feel that there's a row hanging in the air. With no apparent visible signs, we sense that something isn't quite right and quickly work out who we want to avoid. Sometimes our gut instinct tells us to be wary of people, but without evidence, our logical mind overrides it, only for us to conclude some time later that our gut instinct was right after all. I've seen theories that suggest that our brain speedily collects a set of data from our senses and converts this to a decision, but we sense first and use the brain to find evidence to back up what we feel. We develop our emotional radar long before the thinking brain comes into action. This applies to both our evolution and our childhood development. The thinking brain was always a bit of an upgrade.

I recently learnt that babies pick up on their mother's emotions. According to author and therapeutic coach Alex Howard (2021), babies learn to regulate their own nervous system by tuning into the nervous system of their mother. This natural instinct can be risky or beneficial. If a mother doesn't have the skills to soothe her own nervous system, the child won't develop them either. This deep connection and alignment between two separate bodies has to be some form of human Wi-Fi. Howard (2021) also has the capability to tune into the emotions of another, experiencing them as his own. This can be an advantage for healers. Empaths have this ability, but when they don't recognise it, their emotions are running with interference, picking up the signals from everyone around. It can leave them feeling moody without really knowing why. Nurturing self-awareness is powerful. Once I realised that I have the ability to sense the emotions of others, it helped me hone in on my experience, so I could differentiate between my own emotions and someone else's transmission. Most of us believe we're already self-aware but surrounded by people who aren't. We all know people whose traits are so blatantly obvious that we can't believe they're oblivious to them, but is awareness a special gift reserved just for us? Is it possible that these traits sit in our friends' blind spots? If they do, might we as fellow human beings also be afflicted by the same fate? Consider the habits of people we know, such as putting themselves down, talking over others, prying into personal matters with no concept of boundaries or obsessing over the hours that another colleague works. Is it possible that we have a few of our own? When clients tell Howard they aren't anxious, he can feel that they are, even though the clients don't recognise or won't admit to anxiety. Human Wi-Fi is like tuning into someone's energy before they speak.

McKusick (2021), author of *Electric Body Electric Health,* specialises in sound healing. She believes that our body continually vibrates with electric energy resonating at different frequencies. Using forks tuned to the optimum frequency, she can detect the dissonance of blocked energy and re-tune it. Reiki practice focuses on seven spinning vortexes or chakras of life force energy and balancing them for holistic health. Our root chakra grounds us to the earth, whilst our crown chakra connects us with our higher wisdom and universal energy. Chinese medicine traditions believe our energy travels along meridians, each path managing the flow between different parts of the body.

Emoto has studied how music, words and thoughts impact water because the cells in our body are seventy percent salt water. Epigenetics specialist Lipton (2023) suggests that our 53 trillion cells carry a charge that vibrates continuously. Maté (2003) describes diseases such as fibromyalgia as the result of extreme energy losses arising when the body is at a low voltage. This can occur when we're constantly battling internal or external resistance, such as hyperarousal. Maté (2003) suggests we simply run out of charge.

There are so many different holistic approaches that allude to the vibrational energy of the human being. McKusick (2021) provides some insight into how she believes our human connection might work. It was quite by accident that she found out she could re-tune her clients' energy from up to twelve feet away. This prompted her to research what she has now come to label the human biofield, an ether surrounding the body that stores all of our experiences. According to McKusick, the diseases of old emotional events live as energy blocks in this biofield, causing discordance with our environment. Re-tuning our frequencies can bring us back into harmony. She describes this as literally changing our tune. Tolle (2004) also writes that when we don't face strong negative emotions, they become stuck in our energy flow and cause blockages. These frequencies of the human vibration sit outside of our hearing range, which is why they are not immediately obvious. Well, I would say that, wouldn't I? How else could I get away with writing about it in my book? Before that doubt and cynicism takes full hold, I wanted to let you know that there's a machine called the SQUID that can pick up human vibrations from twelve feet away. The superconducting quantum interference device technology was invented in the 1970s and can pick up subtle changes in electromagnetic energy that would otherwise be undetectable. The US HeartMath Institute uses the technology in neurocardiology research. Both the brain and heart give off electromagnetic signals, but the electromagnetic pulse from the heart is believed to be sixty times more powerful than that of the brain. The electric pulses from the body are known as the human biofield, and it interacts with our body, the environment and other people. When we feel like people are invading our personal space, I wonder if they literally are and what happens if they don't resonate on the same frequency as us? Do we get instant dissonance?

This is one of the great principles of Hawkins' (2013) emotional ladder. When he suggests that living without awareness leaves us at the mercy of our default settings, it also has a bearing on who we hang around with. We feel dissonance when we aren't energetically aligned with someone, negatively or positively.

Have you ever noticed how much happy people get on your nerves when you're angry, sad or apathetic? Our default settings can unwittingly influence the people we feel comfortable interacting with. We feel safe in exchanges with like-minded people. I attribute my personal growth to mindfulness, but I recognise that it wasn't always comfortable meeting people that I might not have resonated with in the past. When I worked with the joy team, their approach was very alien to me, and without awareness, I might have shut them out as I'm prone to do when I feel uncomfortable. Once I opened up to this hub of support and friendship, I grew because I overcame some of my historic fears of trusting people. They retaught me how to thrive in a group. When I moved back to a more typical technical environment, it felt alien, like going backwards.

If we're not happy or we feel stuck, we can't imagine what might be possible for us if we're prepared to dip our toe in the water. That's all it takes; we don't have to know what the end looks like because it could be something entirely beyond our current imagination.

We just have to decide that it's time to start. What would good look like in a year? What could we start today to move in that direction? What have we always been drawn to?

Goals and deadlines are great motivators, and I set myself one for the completion of this book, but beware of clinging too tightly. When I first began writing, I was on a Hay House Retreat where they recommended structuring my book proposal into ten chapters.

What came to mind was a half-decent outline for a book of themes, outlining everything I've learnt. When I failed to win their writer's competition and found myself starting again, what came from my heart was a collection of stories that brought all of those themes to life. I went from writing something that was purely factual to telling my story. We can set the course of our general direction, but we must trust in the process and allow things to come to us. This is the great joy of the magical experiences that nature can provide for us.

If we've accepted human evolution in any context, then how can we assume that we've reached the pinnacle of this human path? Hawkins (2013) suggests that we are on the road to increased consciousness and that is our destiny.

Law of Attraction

I'm absolutely convinced that the Tesla car is reproducing itself. There used to be just a few but now I see them everywhere, travelling in pairs so that they can race each other at the traffic lights. I must admit they do shift a little faster than the second most popular electric vehicle—the milk float. Whilst the company was founded in 2003, its brand name is an acknowledgement of the great Nikola Tesla (1856-1943), who invented the induction motor in 1887, making electric vehicles feasible. Unfortunately, there were a number of wealthy advocates heavily invested in oil and fossil fuel, who were quick to point out the dangers of the alternating electrical current. I wonder if this hampered our understanding of the profound nature of electricity because Tesla was a visionary whose ideas stretched far beyond the car. Whilst we cannot be certain of the year, the quote *'If you want to find the secrets of the universe, think in terms of energy, frequency and vibration'* is attributed to Tesla. Within the context of Hawkins' (2013) scale, it makes me wonder if Tesla's understanding of electricity and frequency extended to human beings. Was it possible that he was on the cusp of discovering something truly special? I've seen this quotation many times, but when I tracked it down to Goodreads.com, I found another Tesla quotation, 'My brain is only a receiver, in the Universe there is a core from which we obtain knowledge, strength and inspiration. I have not penetrated into the secrets of this core, but I know that it exists.' He was definitely aware of a higher power and our alignment with it. According to Goodreads.com, Tesla's views weren't widely understood by his peers but were rooted in the ancient traditions that for thousands of years acknowledged the power of sound, vibration and frequency. Tolle (2011) and Hawkins (2013) both refer to a human electrical vibration, but we've lost sight of electricity as a natural resource, mostly understanding it within the context of commercialisation. When we think of human energy, we often link it to the conversion of food into energetic calories. Yet, we're aware of a different flavour of energy, the one that drives our mood and motivation. The principle of the Hawkins emotional energy scale is that human beings do indeed vibrate. The frequency they emit is directly correlated to their emotional state. At the bottom of the scale, the frequency of shame and apathy is slow, ranging from 20 – 40 vibrations. It may be an odd concept, but we've all experienced the lack of energy we feel in these states and, by contrast, the uplifting energy of joy or love.

The prominent theme of the famous book *The Secret,* Byrne (2006) is that everything in the universe vibrates. Within its opening chapters, it reveals that this was understood by the great philosophers and inventors of our time. The book attributes some of their success to their appreciation of the phenomena that we all vibrate and attract to us, people and experiences that resonate on the same vibrational frequency. Some texts suggest that the attraction is based on a connection that's born out of our evolution from a single source, such as an original cell or the universe.

The 13th-century poet and theologian, Rumi, describes human beings as both the ocean and the waves, and Rizvi (2025) describes us as individuals who are also the whole. In his book, *Quantum Manifestation: The Science of Abundance,* he begins by explaining how we view an orange through a prism of glass. No matter how many shards of glass the prism is broken into, each shard still holds the vision of the entire orange. In *The Power of Now,* Tolle (1997) describes the 1982 Aspect Experiment in France. Two particles that began life connected were separated over a vast distance. When one particle was changed, the second changed in the same way. At the time, scientists concluded that the particles were somehow able to connect through a force faster than the speed of light, operating in a higher dimension. Whether this piques your curiosity or you think it's farfetched, just like Wi-Fi in the 1970s, our minds may not be ready for such miracles. Yet nature is a miracle. As you read this book, you're sitting on an Earth that is spinning at around 1,000 miles per hour, faster than the speed of light, which is 767 miles per hour, ThoughtCo.com (2024). For me personally, I feel it's an exciting time to be alive because the holistic and scientific worlds are gravitating closer together. Advances in technology are providing greater research opportunities into the mysteries that surround us.

Hawkins (2013) suggests that our emotions vibrate on a frequency that attracts us to others vibrating at the same level. We've all heard the phrase, 'misery loves company'. Being around someone who's a permanent energy drain is completely different to supporting that close friend going through a rough time. Our emotions ebb and flow, but it's those that stick around or appear most often that become the default setting, which determines our frequency of attraction. Inspirational speaker Tony Robbins also suggests that we have a default setting which surfaces when we feel under threat. Do we have the awareness to step back, or do we run with our programs, becoming instantly angry or shutting down? When someone we know continuously operates at a lower vibrational energy and we tune into our own feelings, we may notice the sensations of dissonance. We might meet them at their frequency, which feels physically draining as we slow down our own vibration. We then expend our energy retuning to our natural state. Alternatively, we spend the entire encounter fighting to keep our energy at our natural buoyancy. Sometimes when there's a large difference between our energy levels, we experience the encounter as someone literally popping our balloon or taking the air out of our sails. Rather than a slowdown, this type of dissonance feels more like a harsh shock to the system. Recognising how we feel in our relationships gives us knowledge that helps us to decide how we use our time and energy. Imagine we spend our afternoon off, listening to the woes of our friend, only to realise that this isn't a one-off, but their habitual state. The encounters leave us feeling drained for several days afterwards, and beforehand, we notice that our body is filled with apprehension and dread. If we're good listeners, people with a lot to offload are naturally drawn to us. As we part company, without thinking, out of habit, duty or politeness, we invite them to meet again next week.

It's mindful awareness that gives us choice in the moment. We can pause and take a step back and not make the usual invitation or make ourselves available. When we're attuned to our experience, we're better able to guard our energy. Clear boundaries help to compartmentalise our experience, ring-fencing the encounter so it's contained to the hours we meet. We can also use Reiki techniques to protect our energy states. The worst-case scenario is that we're empaths without awareness. This makes us susceptible to absorbing the lower emotional frequencies of another and then expending our energy trying to get ourselves back on track. As we move through the stages of growth, we may find that our relationships become incompatible, and people distance themselves from us. When we align with a more peaceful frequency, we find it difficult to get involved in unnecessary drama, meeting it instead with suggestions on how it might be avoided. The person addicted to drama doesn't want advice but resonates more easily with the attentive friend who hangs on every word of their story, eager for the next instalment.

We must also be mindful of our struggle with raising our emotional frequency. As we grow and navigate more towards people on a higher vibration, we initially experience dissonance. The vibration of someone who's more joyful or accepting of situations may feel strange to be around, so our self-protecting ego will create a story for us. Maybe we conclude that they've had an easy life and have no idea of the sort of struggles we've faced. This might be true because when we start on our journey of life, we are content. It's our experiences that shape our emotional path for better or worse, but we have no proof that their journey has been easier. Even if it has, we are here to explore ourselves, and the sort of comparison that dips into our sense of victimhood isn't helpful. Dissonance can be a gift because it's a sign that we feel out of alignment with the current situation. Whilst our mind can influence how we feel, our true interpretation is stored in the physical sensations of the body. We can feel conflicted as part of us wants to grow and may even aspire to become more like this person we're not resonating with. Meanwhile, another part of us feels much safer exactly where we are.

Physicist and organisational leader Lex Sisney applies the laws of physics to our energetic experiences, describing dissonance as a friction that forces us to expend more energy than we need to, in pursuit of an activity. Sisney suggests, *'We all have a finite amount of energy over time.'* Chaotic actions spread our energy randomly across multiple pursuits, resulting in very little progress. Bringing order and a razor-sharp focus creates the pleasurable experience of energetic flow, where even the process becomes enjoyable. A firm sense of direction helps us to overcome the distractions that arise. Alternatively, pursuing but not finishing multiple tasks is frustrating and prevents us from realising that sense of achievement. When we experience the reward of achieving, we become organically energised as the body releases the hormones of dopamine and oxytocin. The latter is more likely to encourage us to rest and reflect on our accomplishments. The body has its own way of rewarding us and topping up our energy supplies, once we understand its operating system.

In the world of personal growth, there's a very fine line to tread between setting a firm goal and creating enough flexibility to be open to experiences that may arise along the way. If we imagine setting off from London with the intention of getting to Edinburgh on a single tank of fuel, we'll likely look at the shortest and most exact route. No one loves a quaint country cottage more than I do, but if we mindlessly drift from one historic village to the next, we burn up our fuel without reaching our destination. These diversions represent the friction that compromises our energy supply, making life a little bit more taxing than it needs to be. If we reflect on our initial goal and decide that visiting the villages contributes to our overall objective, we can set a new intention that makes this part of the journey. The subtlety is whether or not we choose the diversion. This is what Brown (2018) and Doyle (2020) refer to as getting deliberate in our lives. The challenge is that we have moved from a pull to a push society. In the past, we sought out the information we wanted, pulling it towards us when we needed to. Now we are bombarded with MSN stories with enticing hooks, clickbait, emails and course ideas that take us down multiple rabbit holes. Some of these distractions are useful, but in the past, we decided when and whether we sought them out. They tap into our fear of missing out, and whilst we're dealing with the distractions, our priorities are getting pushed further down the list. It may seem like we're off track for just a few minutes, but how we spend an hour becomes how we spend a week and then before we know it, how we spend a lifetime.

Whilst distractions can deplete our energy, our inner world, particularly our desire to feel safe, can also block our progress. Thoughts and beliefs can debilitate us, leaving us drained in a state of apathy and requiring great energetic will to move on. Hidden beliefs and automatic coping strategies, left unattended, become our internal saboteurs. If we've only ever travelled up the M6 in a northerly direction on a Friday evening, we might have a belief that all motorways are congested, and the most effective route is via the A roads. Someone who has only travelled during the day via the M6 toll road will have a completely different view. Neither conclusion is incorrect, but both have reached an assumption based on a narrow focus of information, captured at a point in time. When we unwittingly take this as fact, it informs our narrative, and we accept it as a belief that we might never question again. These beliefs drive, sidetrack, de-motivate, or just leave us stuck in a stale old story. Life coach Mia Hewett has a nifty way of challenging such beliefs, and it's through one simple statement, "If it's true for me, it must be true for everyone." Beliefs are harder to identify and unpick when they're shared by our immediate community. If we grow up in a setting where people have always struggled with money, then we'll believe that money is difficult to find and reject any evidence to the contrary. For example, we think that education will give us better opportunities, but when we finish college and see an ideal role with an attractive salary, we talk ourselves out of the application process. We may have the skills, but we don't believe that people like us are offered these positions. We block ourselves before we've even tried. The classic school mantra of money being directly linked to hard work isn't what we think it is.

I've juggled multiple responsibilities in small companies, adding tremendous value to the bottom line. Yet I've been better financially rewarded for doing less, in bigger companies with a better budget. Salary can be linked to the company's ability to pay, not just the effort we put into the role. Care work is one of the most mentally and physically challenging roles in our society. Often, the pay is just above minimum wage and has no bearing on the hard work required. If work and money were directly correlated in the way we've come to believe, this situation would not exist.

There are people who break free from their default mould, reaching success that goes way beyond the expectations of their initial start in life. Sometimes they're ostracised or mocked for 'getting ideas above their station'. This is because when our beliefs keep us stuck, we feel comfortable being the victim of our circumstances. Once one person demonstrates the art of the possible, staying stuck becomes a choice that we have to take accountability for. Brown (2018) reminds us that the arena is full of people throwing criticism from the cheap seats. If we want advice on personal growth, are we going to listen to those people who are stuck, or those who are in the arena fighting for their cause? It can be helpful to find a cheerleader who's further along a similar path.

Beliefs appear to be of the mind, but we feel them in the body, and they set the emotional frequency that attracts our experience. Positive thinking can sometimes lift our mood, but there's a fine line between improving how we feel and riding roughshod over those feelings that usually have something to tell us. If we have a deep-rooted belief that we deserve to be poor, no amount of positive thinking about attracting wealth will be able to override this sense. When our perception is that attracting money is a problem, we broadcast the emotional vibration of struggling. Low self-esteem also leaves us vibrating with the sensations of lack and blocking our access to higher frequencies, because our body can't get behind ambitious plans if our self-belief is lacking. The situations that work naturally for me are those that I don't question because I have no problem believing in their possibility. Throw away comments such as, "I could do with that letter arriving this week" or "I could do with the road being clear so I can get off the drive," all fall into place. Those experiences hold no emotional baggage, telling me that I'm undeserving or asking for the impossible. Success arrives when the statement is very specific; it includes a what or when but aligns with what I physically believe is possible for me.

When my project got cancelled and I needed a new contract, I kept the usual fear of lack at bay, trusting that something would turn up. It took awareness to keep my reactions in check so I could tap into courage and self-reassurance. I recognised the natural emotions of fear nagging at the base of my stomach and acknowledged that whilst they were understandable in the circumstances, they didn't need to become my truth. Within days, the friend I was meeting for coffee had an opportunity for me. Raising our vibrational frequency is not just about thinking we deserve something but feeling it.

We can't buy our esteem like designer brands or beauty procedures, much like we can't prop it up with academic qualifications. Yet, we are all equally deserving of the best that life has to offer and cultivating a felt sense of this belief is the foundation of unrooting debilitating patterns. According to Dr Kristen Neff (2011), self-esteem places a value on our social positioning, leaving us vying for status in place of recognising our equality. The Dalai Lama has no concept of self-esteem or low self-worth, Davidson & Begley (2012). It doesn't exist within their culture because it's a mental and cultural creation in the mind. Seeing emotions for what they are helps us to create space to be with their ebb and flow. We all have challenges, but it's our tendency to over-identify with our experience that can make emotions sticky and persistent. When someone suggests we are 'glass half empty', they're not differentiating between our emotional state and who we are, but when we're able to separate the two, it's empowering. We are more than our emotions, and they don't need to define us. Nipping to the loo is a fantastic analogy which I picked up from one of my teachers. Have you ever gone for a giant poo, looked down the loo and defined yourself by that mushy brown lump that exited your body? Absolutely not! There's no doubt in our minds that this is just something passing through us, and this is the way to experience our emotions. Just like your poo, they will pass through. I experience my emotions; they do not define me.

The sense of separation we can achieve through mindful awareness can make it more palatable to explore those emotions that don't quite align with who we think we are. When we see ourselves as a calm person, anger is out of alignment, so we might be tempted to suppress it, but denying our emotions is denying part of our experience. When we don't honour how we feel, we invalidate our reality, and that can lead to self-resentment. We have less control than we think over which emotions arise, but in order to grow, we need to be with them all. The antidote is the self-compassion that arises when we can meet our suffering with kindness, Chödrön (2002) and any situation that leaves us at the mercy of self-sabotaging, self-destruction is a form of suffering. The practice of kindness visualisations influences our neural pathways and, according to Emoto (2004) and Lipton (2023), the very cells that make up our human body. This is how we start feeling differently and learning to accept that we, too, deserve kindness. Through compassion-based self-acceptance, the inner beliefs of poor self-worth begin to dwindle, bringing us closer to the human miracle that we truly are. When a baby is born, the miracle of their life is enough. It's the cultural stories and demands we must meet to retain that love, which creates the life's work for the ego. Authentic self-acceptance is equal and doesn't come at the expense of others. It's unconditional and it doesn't care how we look or age, what we achieve or how we are seen by others, because when we recognise the nature of our human fallibility, we realise that the ideal sense of self that we've worked so hard to protect, never really existed. It didn't exist for us and doesn't exist for anyone else. We're all presenting our perfect sense of self to the world and denying each other the opportunity to be authentic in the process. In recognising our own fallibility, we see that of the human race.

In recognising our own pain and illusions, we see the collective suffering. Acknowledging our common humanity opens up our sense of a shared connection. Compassion and kindness are not just about being nice, they lay the foundations for the skills of neutrality, acceptance and joy. These emotions help us to resonate at the higher frequencies of emotional consciousness, bringing us into alignment with new experiences. The more we access these higher frequencies, the stronger the connected neural pathways become. Our vibration will still move through states of Tigger and Eeyore, but with mindful awareness, the hope is that we can channel our inner Pooh and tap into our higher wisdom. We're all in this together, sharing this human experience and vibrating through our emotional rollercoaster. It is through the awareness and compassion for ourselves and humanity that we're able to transcend Hawkins (2013) emotional energy scale. Mindfulness is the vehicle that makes this possible.

It's Not Your Fault

What continually drew me to mindfulness were those kind, safe voices. Turn on a recording of Thich Nhat Hanh, Tara Brach or Jack Kornfield and you'll hear the warmth and compassion in their voices. They truly walk their walk, offering unconditional compassion to all because underneath whatever stories we tell ourselves, we're all human beings deserving of peace and love. When I started learning to meditate, it was these voices that made me feel safe, and I knew I'd experienced the type of world I wanted to live in. It was confusing and reassuring. Physically, I was safe. It was my inner world which kept me on the lookout for threats. Sadly, many of those came from inside my own head. If there was a difficult way to navigate something, I would find it, because surely, we can only be rewarded for what we have truly earned.

When we unpack the lives of inspirational people, their stories often include pain and adversity, so once again we are reminded of the beautiful lotus flower that blooms not despite the mud but because of it. When I look at the life I have lived so far, I've always considered it to be somewhat of an oogie, googie mess. I know there are friends who think that this constant re-invention is inspirational, but it's truly been born out of escaping one situation after another. Only now do I realise, we can't outrun ourselves, at some point we have to turn up and dance to our own tune. Our emotions drift in and out but until we can recognise the stories they tell us, we live at their mercy, hiding in fear and thinking that safety lies somewhere else. We get stuck in a loop of conflicting ideas where that desire to escape butts up against the fear that everywhere else will be just the same and yes, it will be! If we are the same, then our experiences form a pattern until we are ready to be different. Changing the outer world looks great at the start as we bask in our honeymoon period. We truly want to believe that we've made a better choice, so we notice those experiences that validate that we made the right move. We ignore the little problems along the way until, just like every other situation we've ever been in, the small things become the big things. Slowly, it dawns on us that we've landed in a career or relationship that looks the same as everything we've escaped before. This doesn't have to be our destiny.

This is fear-based living, where we escape versus choosing because our program tells us that we need to do enough to survive, but it isn't just your program, it's the human experience. It's one we've been practising for billions of years. This is the DNA of humanity, and our ancestors entangle it with the flavours of their life experiences. In her book *Emotional Alchemy*, Bennett-Goleman (2002) suggests that true healing acknowledges the wounds of three generations. That's a lot of pain to mop up, but reflecting on the struggles of our ancestors can provide the context for our own pain. When our Nan passes judgement on something we do and we roll our eyes to the ceiling, we're getting an insight into her inner world and the standards by which she measures herself. My nan was very disappointed in me when, at nineteen years old, I was 'living over the brush'. These were her words to describe two people living together before they are married.

I wasn't quick enough to pick up on the hypocrisy, but simply reduced myself to the smallness we experience when we're shamed by our grandparents. Nan never married and spent most of her early adult life living with her mother in a small village in Liverpool. She had two children out of wedlock. I imagine that during the 1950s, my nan felt the full weight of judgement in that small village, and it probably tapped into those primal fears of banishment from the tribe. Whilst Nan was judged for her actions, the person who felt the true force was her daughter, my mum. She was the one who was shamed for simply being born, the unloved mistake. She never said, but I know it stuck with her, undermining her self-worth. My mum's one wish for me was that I never end up like her—a single mum with three children. It saddens me to the core that this is all she saw in herself. When I talk about the experiences that have shaped my life, I have only respect for this resilient woman who raised her family in very difficult circumstances. All of the strength I have comes from this strong, funny woman who lived and laughed despite her own pain. I wish I had the chance to tell Mum that she didn't fail at life and that we love her in a way her own mother just didn't have the capacity to do.

When I talk of my own pain, I recognise that for me, fear has been a motivator. I was about thirty-five when my hypnotherapist quoted Aristotle, 'Show me the child of seven and I'll show you the man.' It frightened me. Knowing what I know of my childhood, I didn't want my life to be shaped by the emotional energy of that seven-year-old. When someone says, "You can't," my gut reaction is: watch me! So, when my book proposal was rejected by Hay House, it was their response that became the catalyst for writing this book. It's not my life's work to alter this fear-based motivation, but understanding my operating system is powerful. With awareness of this driving fear, I can overcome the urge to step on a beautiful ring to save face and can also leverage that painful book rejection to motivate me to write. Unrecognised fear can drive behaviour that initially looks positive but can lead us to destructive patterns of behaviour, such as the way we strive for that promotion or recognition.

When I set myself a target of getting promoted within two years, I could have walked into my manager's office and set out my stall, making my ambitions clear. What I didn't realise at the time was that I had a deep-seated fear of being rejected that made this impossible. On some level, I doubted my own ability and worried about the day I'd bump into that person who was happy to spell out my failures. Fear of failure, fear of not being good enough, all tapping into those primal worries of being banished from the tribe.

I'd never have to face this risk, because I had my own way of doing things. I'd simply work harder, take on additional projects and more responsibility. I'd show everyone how capable I truly was. After all, isn't this what we're taught? Initially, I was high on the adrenaline of success, but at some point, I realised my plan wasn't working. This is when all of that enthusiasm tipped over into resentment. Mostly, I directed it towards the manager who had all of the kudos I desired, but not, in my opinion, any of the skills or acumen for the position. Work became completely impossible.

I struggled so much with the dynamics of working for him that the hairs on the back of my neck would stand up every time he moved from his chair. My mind went into overdrive trying to imagine what lunacy he was about to inflict on me. I can't say in true faith that I underestimated his incompetence and genuinely still believe that my hard work and skills contributed to his own outward appearance of success. So why would he promote me when everything was going so well for him? I kept fixing and filling in the gaps, becoming more obsessed with his behaviour. I took on responsibilities that truly sat with him and blamed him for my actions. Whilst I was looking at him and feeling like a victim, I couldn't take responsibility for myself. We forget that other people have their own path to tread, and when we get too caught up in theirs, we lose sight of our own. It is the challenges in life that we remember, as they often help us to grow. Each time we fix something for someone else, we take that opportunity from them. We may even leave them feeling stuck or helpless, tapping into their own sense of victimhood. It's a complete misdirection of our energy. This was the path I followed, not through choice but because it was the only way I knew how to operate. What if I had spelt out what I wanted for myself? I might have faced some difficult answers but here's the thing. Sometimes we know that we have more to offer, and when the beliefs of the people who can make this happen for us aren't aligned with ours, this is empowering. Yes, we can interpret this as a failure because we want to fit in and be recognised but we're not here to live up to the expectations of others. If we're not valued, we don't have to stay, but we have to believe that we deserve to be fulfilled, whatever that looks like for us. It turned out that it usually took around four years to get the promotion I was determined to pull off in two. I'm only just coming to terms with the painful fact that many of my self-expectations have little bearing in reality.

Becoming aware of my unrealistic expectations took me back to being fourteen years old when I came across an offer in one of those Sunday magazines. Britannia Music Club used to advertise attractive offers on books and records. The customer would apply for the offer, unwittingly entering into a subscription to the album of the month. Whilst the offer album might be from a well-known artist like the Rolling Stones, the next album of the month would be something obscure, such as the best of Sefton and Bartholomew! The latter are actually good musicians, but I'm still smarting from the disappointment of my lucky find at a car boot sale. I was thrilled to discover *The Best of Simon and Garfunkel* at a bargain price, but a little perplexed that they didn't sound quite right. Song after song, I sat there wondering what was amiss until I eventually noticed that right there on the cover, in the bottom left-hand corner and in the tiniest writing possible, it said sung by Sefton and Bartholomew. I never fell for the album of the month subscription again, but was intrigued by an entire course on how to improve your memory. It was expensive and I literally didn't have a bean, but Britannia offered a fourteen-day money-back guarantee, so I figured that I could read it within the trial period and then send it back. I filled out the form, sent it off by freepost and then waited in eager anticipation. Unfortunately, when this magic course finally turned up, it was a collection of seven books!

Not one to let facts or realism get in the way, I set myself the goal of reading one book every two days. When my plan failed, I increased my reading time to complete one book per day. Eventually, I sent the books back, having managed to get through the first two. I was disappointed in myself, not for setting unrealistic expectations, but for not being able to read seven books in fourteen days. Ouch! This is the crazy mind I'm working with, and this is what we get to see when we cultivate self-awareness. These expectations can become obsessive, and when we tie them in with fear of failure, we become trapped in the cycle of the threat and drive system, just as Gilbert outlines in his emotional model. Without any hope of completing our impossible task, we fail to reach any sort of closure, depriving ourselves of the reward hormones that top up our energy. When we think we're failing, we throw time at the problem, missing out on those activities that bring us joy and also top up our contentment hormones. As we live on adrenaline, our body fights hard to return us to a state of balance. Kristen Neff describes this as fighting both sides of our own internal argument, with different parts of the body competing against each other, so we're working twice as hard.

Self-awareness is tricky, particularly if we start to try and correct our operating system. The approach becomes a paradox because when we turn on our inner fear-based world, with criticism, we just generate more fear. One of my great teachers, Choden, leads a guided compassion meditation for the inner critic using the words, "It's not our fault." This complex human experience has been shaped by all of humanity, and so much of what we beat ourselves up for sits outside of our control. This is why we have to learn to approach our experience and inner world with compassion. Those fear-based emotions will still arise, and it might be tempting to push them aside as we strive to attain the emotional vibrations above courage. Ironically, it's our ability to allow all of our experiences to be just as they are that actually raises our energetic vibration. When we acknowledge those parts of us that don't live up to the lofty expectations of the ego, we are literally practising acceptance. This practice gently steers us away from the fear-based narrative that keeps us trapped below courage. Our emotional vibration will never be black or white, because emotions will always come and go, but we can shift the percentages in our favour by turning towards our experiences with kindness.

On some level, we believe we are solely responsible for our own survival, and this can lead us to strive towards perfectionism as we hustle to keep our place in the tribe. Our individualistic culture still pits us against each other, and therefore, the faults we don't want to see are the flaws we imagine will lead to expulsion. When we live in fear, we live in lack, and survival is paramount at any cost. This fear-based narrative can make it difficult for us to meet people where they are, particularly if we are apprehensive of new relationships. The great paradox of facing into our own experience is that the nature of being human begins to dawn, and we recognise that our stories are the stories of humanity. The chapters might be longer or shorter, but fundamentally, we are all on the same path facing the collective challenges of this human experience.

As our consciousness rises above courage, we're better able to work for the greater good. No longer compelled to stick within the comfort of our tribe, we recognise that humanity is our tribe. When we use mindfulness to build awareness of our experience, we can begin to let go of our need to defend the ego, and by relaxing this self-protection, we open up to deep, heartfelt connections with others. Finding the courage to move through this fear truly does lead to new horizons, new people, new experiences and beautiful energy.

Vino Rosso'd

So here we are at the last chapter. For months, I've been hammering away at the keys, refining the second part of the book, motivated by a goal to finish it before I go off to Italy on retreat. I've worked solidly perfecting a couple of chapters every week, and whilst I've tried to enjoy the process, rather than fixating on the goal, facing my own grand expectations has been the real challenge. When I sat down hoping to box off a chapter a day, followed by a five-mile walk, what I expected to take a couple of hours usually took eight. Once again, realism felt like the dark enemy stripping the joy from my soul.

With three days to go until my departure, I finished the penultimate chapter. Oh, I was so close. I mulled over the challenge of completing the last chapter before smugly flying off to the retreat. I could almost picture myself levitating in Yodaesque style above my sun lounger, as I waxed lyrical about completing my book. Firstly, I cannot levitate. I knew you'd be wondering about that, and secondly, I'm terrible at self-recognition. More importantly, I'd spent the last few months refining already written chapters, and at this stage, the last chapter was merely a collection of notes.

With fear of failure lurking, I knew I could pull a few long nights and get it finished, but I also knew it would leave me feeling completely washed out on the retreat.

I'm by no means the finished article, but somewhere inside me, a deeper wisdom prevailed. Within the pages of this book, I've aired the good, the bad and the ugly and reading it back, I've laughed, cried, winced and worried. This wasn't a chapter to be rushed. It needed reflection and time. I needed to tell you that it works out okay, and hopefully send you on your way a little bit inspired. This was a chapter to curate during and after the retreat. Also, how fitting would it be to end the book just as I opened it, on retreat. This is the irony of slowing down to move forward, the classic tale of the tortoise and the hare. When we step away from the noise, there is wisdom beneath. We don't need to wrestle with the waves, we can go deep below the ocean surface, into that vast space where things become a little slower, calmer and clearer. Goals can be effective, but sometimes we need to allow things to unfold organically, doing things the right way, not the quickest. This mindful approach to life goes against the very core of my striving, achieving default setting. But seeing our operating system is everything, as we get to uncover what we are truly working with.

The power of mindfulness can be so poorly interpreted, as illustrated by the young girl I overheard in a lift in Liverpool Central Station. She said, "Mindfulness is supposed to make me feel calm, but it pisses me off." These are the expectations that we bump into when we try to meditate or be more mindful. My lovely yoga teacher, Dr Amanda Bowen, describes meditation as the time we spend with ourselves. It's a powerful analogy after all; this is the longest relationship we'll have, but it's one we don't prioritise. So, whose life are you living right now?

It is in our aloneness that we truly discover what we need, and it can be difficult to pin that down, particularly when we spend our time buffering up the lives of everyone else. Being alone is the only way to find out who we are, because in this process, there is no compromise; it really is just us. Meditation doesn't need to be your starting point; we can try something as simple as defining the perfect day and being playful in our quest. Try it for a few hours and see how it works out. Remind yourself who you were before life got in the way. Journaling is also very powerful when we let go of expectations and stop getting too caught up in sense-checking every word. We can use simple prompts such as "I love it when", "I feel amazing when" or "Joy is…", allowing the words to flow through us onto the page. It's a brain splurge rather than an academic test. When our words flow freely, the mind and soul pour out our deepest yearnings. Follow them up, test them out and see what it is that truly lifts your soul. You may find out that being with others is better for you, but the point of being alone is that you find the answers, and this can be freeing.

I'm opening and closing this book with retreats, and even to myself, it sounds idyllic. If you follow the work of Bruce Lipton, you'll appreciate his views on how our environment powerfully influences us at a cellular level. He also explains how our thoughts and emotions create our inner environment. Some of those stories we play out have been around for a long time. It doesn't matter how perfect that retreat escape looks; all of those stories come with us until we see them for what they are and allow them to fade away. My first retreat on Holy Isle was in 2019 and was part of the Aberdeen master's degree and the Mindfulness Association's teaching program. Much like joining Chester College because it had a swimming pool, the Holy Isle retreat had really piqued my interest when I was considering mindfulness courses.

The journey to Holy Isle starts with a ferry trip from Stranraer to Arran followed by a short bus ride around to the other side of the island. Here, a smaller boat ferries passengers across to Holy Isle. It's a beautiful location, mountainous, green and occupied by wild goats, horses and birdlife. With amazing views across the sea, I felt at home immediately, but I almost didn't make it to the retreat. I'd been apprehensive that I'd be trapped on an island with people I didn't know, overwhelmed with a desire to escape. On the edge of the island, there's a beautiful wooden seating area on the banks of the North Sea. It was here that we began our teaching journey, each of us leading different sections of the same meditation. We had a rough idea that everyone would lead for five minutes, but when we closed our eyes and settled into that space, it felt like we were gently passing a baton from one person to another, each person sensing the subtleties of a pause and picking up the guidance. It was a deep, powerful, flowing connection that felt special and stayed with me. The teaching retreats were interrupted by Covid, and we never got a chance to go back, so when I discovered a yoga retreat on the island, I was excited to return. This time, there were no fears of escape. However, as I checked the timetable the week before, I noticed there were more yoga sessions than I'd expected. My preference is slow yoga, and I find it easier to connect with those teachers who allow you to actually find your pose before moving on to the next.

I have grim memories of attending a faster-paced yoga class during my lunch hour in Manchester. My colleague and I just couldn't keep up and ended up lying on the floor snorting with laughter. Meanwhile, the rest of the class continued like the true adults they were. The more I thought about the retreat timetable, the more I obsessed about those slim, athletic people, poised carefully in their tree poses. I worried that my fitness would let me down, or I wouldn't have the right clothes. Then, of course, my arms would be flailing around all over the place as I tried to keep my balance. I was beginning to wonder if I'd been a little hasty with my booking, and as I waited for the ferry at Stranraer, I was convinced that I should have just booked a holiday with my husband, like every normal person does. Fortunately, it turned out that once again the experience was nothing like I'd imagined. The group was filled with people of all ages and abilities. There were retired couples, teachers and Reiki healers. The whole of life gathered right there in that beautiful place, talking, laughing and sharing the experience. Amongst the silence and the meditations, I had a small epiphany.

I'd arrived at the retreat expecting judgement from the outside world when, in actual fact, all of the harsh criticism had been right there in my head all along. No one judges me as harshly as myself.

So here I am heading to retreat number three with a missing book chapter lurking on my to-do list. I've met the teacher, I've flown alone before, and I'm a mindfulness coach. I've got this covered. I'm looking forward to a night alone on the island before we meet as a group and the place is absolutely gorgeous. As I settle into my sea view, I wonder whether it's too early to put on the fluffy bathrobe and read on the bed, but I know I need to eat. Suddenly, I'm that child in the corner, seen but alone. My body remembers the college days of eating in my room because I couldn't face eating alone or approaching others. I'm surprised to find myself back here, particularly with all of the personal work I've done. I love people watching in coffee shops, but restaurants are different. It's here that I feel the eyes of the world upon me, pitying the woman with no friends. I know it's a story, but it doesn't stop me staring at the complimentary crisps in my room and wondering if two bags will be enough for my evening meal.

I decide to go out walking and find somewhere to eat. The restaurant by the hotel is open but I can't see inside, and it puts me off. I walk further up the hill and find a restaurant that looks like it's about to open, so I continue walking, promising myself I'll nip in on the way back. When I circle back, there are glamourous couples arriving and many of the tables are reserved. As my nerves kick in, I bolt like a frightened deer heading back to my room, but I know I want to overcome this, so I consider trying the restaurant by the hotel. Bravely tapping into my extensive vocabulary of around fifteen Italian words, I say good evening and ask for a table for one. The host smiles warmly and asks if I'd like a Dutch menu or an English one! Oh, dear, they're onto me. As I take the English menu, she leads me to a table where I awkwardly and quickly plonk myself down. She kindly suggests that I swap seats to take in the beautiful sea view, and it is beautiful.

People continue eating, wrapped up in their own conversations. They barely give a second glance to the English woman eating alone. I order a large beer, take in the view and physically sigh. The next day, I make it to a solo breakfast and a solo dip in the cold seawater pool. I hate cold water, but I tell myself that I might never have another opportunity to climb into this gorgeous spa pool overlooking the sea. This discomfort I've braced myself for lasts a mere five seconds. The staff from my yoga hotel come to collect me. They're a friendly family who really cannot do enough for us, and I feel relaxed meeting my yoga buddies for the first time.

The retreat host has kindly included a meal in Sant'Angelo and the hotel staff, taxi us down. Whilst we laugh and connect over yoga, it's during these evening meals that we get to know each other. The red wine drinkers, the pudding lovers and the reasons for coming on the retreat. I still have that lurking fear of meeting people floating around in my mind, but at last I see my stories for what they are and decide that it's time to write new ones. How we feel emotionally impacts how we interact and who we want to be around. It also signals to others so that they can decide if they want to spend time with us. Fear-based emotions can resonate as pride, arrogance or withdrawal, but each time we challenge a fear-based habit, we weaken its neural pathway. This is how we open our hearts and summon up the courage to step out of our comfort zone, adopting more of an approach style of behaviour. When we do, we get to meet some amazing people. It's a beautiful evening by the bay, relaxing over a glass of red wine and getting to know more about the lives of these gorgeous women. These are women who, like me, seem better able to self-deprecate than to self-congratulate. They worry about the demands on their time and fear they'll run out of road before achieving everything that lives in their head. There are no egos to protect here, just pure, authentic honesty. We weren't meant to shut ourselves away, tackling our battles independently, because our fight is everyone's fight, and when we see our own stories in those of other people, we're moved by our common humanity. We recognise that we're part of something much bigger, and this becomes available to us when we authentically connect with like-minded people. If being around people leaves us feeling isolated and alone, then those people aren't our tribe. People who cannot open their hearts to us have their own stories to deal with. It's not our responsibility to delve too deeply into their world, even if we think understanding their issues will validate our feelings of rejection. We can never completely know another's journey, or that of the three generations they descended from. So, we take responsibility for our own energy and allow others to look after their own. We don't need to analyse every fear story, because the courage to rise above them allows us to tip the emotional energy in a new direction. This is the nature of the inner work, and as we move more towards willingness and acceptance, we naturally raise our level of consciousness and our emotional vibration. We become more Tigger than Eeyore with a measure of Pooh thrown in for guidance.

All emotions have their place, and fear will always be there to keep us safe. We must honour this emotion but allow it to pass through when it needs to, recognising that the power of acceptance moves us to a higher vibrational energy where we can learn to thrive. This is our optimum state and it's what we all truly deserve. As our awareness builds and we make different choices, our neural pathways strengthen around those choices, allowing the paths to the old stories and lower emotional states to weaken and fall away. Mindfulness not only builds our self-awareness, but it also has the power to change the neural pathways and grey matter within the brain. We've experienced the fear-based narrative for too long, and it's left people feeling broken and excluded. It's time for love, connection and joy. This is the only hustle I'm happy to take part in.

The joy that lifts our energy even from the depths of despair is all around us in nature. It's the chuckle of a baby, the song of the blackbird, the purr of the cat or the wag of the dog's tail. The flower doesn't run to the bee for fear of missing out; it trusts in the power of the well-coordinated miracle that is nature. It plays its part in the beautiful orchestra along with the birds, the seeds and the trees. We, too, are part of this miracle, but we need to change our focus from seeking out the fear and tuning into what nature has provided for us. I know which world I want to live in. It's one that I couldn't have imagined for myself even seven years ago. I recognise the challenges that have shaped my life, but in coming face to face with my own demons, I realise that we all have our own demons to face. We are all part of this emotional mess, trying to make sense of the world.

When we find our people, the story of connection becomes clear and it is comforting, warm and welcoming. As we leave the restaurant in Sant'Angelo and make our way back up the hill, we are high on the joys of life and maybe a little red wine. The manager from our hotel waits politely for the seven bubbly women to arrive and I search my fifteen-word dictionary in the hope of offering him an explanation. I have no words, so I improvise. "I'm sorry, we're vino rosso'd." As he smiles and opens the door, Jane turns to me and says, "I think he knows."

So, this has been my mindfulness journey so far. Some of my fear stories still lurk but I see them and get to choose how I rewrite them. I even have an 'I'll just retrain as a plumber' story, which haunts me when I can't get things done within my timescales. These ego tantrums still arise when things aren't going my way, but now I recognise that the very deadlines that rule our lives are often built on false notions that have no real depth beyond a childish whim. There are many players in the orchestra, and we were not made to play every part. Just as we trade our skills for money, so do others. Paying people for their support is part of an energetic financial exchange, and the world wouldn't work if we all kept our money in our bank account because it was cheaper or quicker to do everything ourselves. When we buy from a local business, we're supporting someone's desire to live their life authentically, following their aspirations.

In exchange, we gain the miracle resource of time to spend as we wish. This exchange creates our space for just being, whatever that looks like for us.

I'm still possessed by the terrible trio, striving, impatience and fixing but I know I'm part of something much bigger and there's a place for everyone, even those people we can't quite gel with. It's often these uncomfortable encounters that have the most to teach us. Friends and foes have helped me along the way, and I bear no ill towards the people I have mentioned in the book. Bumping into others is part of our growth. No matter how many hours we spend on the mat, it's interacting with people that really sets those inner processes in motion. Some train by sitting in silence for days or even months, but that has not been my journey.

Mindfulness has taught me that I'm not broken after all. It's given me the strength not to control but to trust in something far bigger than myself. This is where the work lies for me. The emotional scale that I've tracked in the book will take us all the way up to the dizzy heights of enlightenment, and I like to think that for mere mortals like us, we can take that on as a lighter way to live. When we engage more frequently with the higher energetic emotions, according to Hawkins, their power multiplies. Someone demonstrating joy and unconditional love for all can influence the energy of thousands of people. We observe this when we're in the presence of calm, influential souls such as the Dalai Lama, Mother Theresa or Thich Nhat Hanh. Hawkins is taking us along the path of ascension into a higher consciousness, a journey that he believes to be part of our human evolution. When I read *Origin* by Dan Brown, I realised that we already believe we're at the top of our evolutionary tree, but this goes against the very principle of evolution. This transcension is not a linear path and is one that, according to Buddhist philosophy, might take multiple lifetimes.

In this lifetime, I get to publish a book and I'm tired, excited and petrified all at the same time. I really don't know if I'm ready to put it out there because telling my story has been such a personal process, but it's a story that needs to be told because it's so much bigger than me. Somewhere in the pages of my story is your story and everyone else's. I've talked about using courage to overcome fear and to allow our soul energy to burst through, creating a life where we can truly thrive. This is the story of *The Emotional Hustle*.

References

BBC (2002 to Current), *Escape to the Country.* London: BBC Television Studio.

BENNETT-GOLEMAN, T. (2002) *Emotional Alchemy: How the Mind Can Heal the Heart.* New York: Three Rivers Press.

BROWN, B. (2010) *The Gifts of Imperfection.* Minnesota: Hazelden.

BROWN, B. (2018) *Dare to Lead*. London: Vermillion.

BROWN, B. (2021) *Atlas of the Heart*. London: Vermillion.

BROWN, D. (2018) *Origin.* London: Corgi.

BYRNE, R. (2006) *The Secret.* London: Simon & Schuster.

CENTRE FOR MENTAL HEALTH (2018) *Mental health problems at work cost UK economy £34.9bn last year.* Online: https://www.centreformentalhealth.org.uk/news/mental-health-problems-work-cost-uk-economy-ps349bn-last-year-says-centre-mental-health. Accessed: October 2020.

CHODEN, REGAN-ADDIS, H. (2017) *Mindfulness Association: Mindfulness Based Living Course.* Hampshire: John Hunt Publishing.

CHODRON, P. (1994) *Start Where You Are: A Guide to Compassionate Living*. Boston: Shambhala.

CHODRON, P. (2002) *The Places That Scare You: A Guide to Fearlessness in Difficult Times.* Audible: Shambhala.

CLEESE, J.; BOOTH, C. (1997) *Fawlty Towers: Communication Problems.* London: BBC Television Centre.

DAHL, C.J; LUTZ, A; DAVIDSON, R. (2015) *Reconstructing and deconstructing the self: cognitive mechanisms in meditation practice.* Trends in Cognitive Sciences, Volume 19.9.

DAVIDSON, R. J; BEGLEY, S. (2012) *The Emotional Life of Your Brain. How its unique patterns affect the way you think, feel, and live – and how you can change them.* New York: Hudson Street Press.

DAMASIO, A. (2000) *The Feeling of What Happens.* Boston: Mariner Books.

DOYLE, G. (2020) *Untamed.* London: Vermillion.

DYER, W. (2024) *Master the Art of Manifesting: Live Lecture.* California: Hay House LLC.

DWECK, C.S. (2019) *Mindset: Changing the Way You Think to Fulfil Your Potential.* Audio: Hachette Audio UK.

EMOTO, M. (2004) *The Hidden Messages In Water.* London: Simon Schuster Audio.

FIELDING, H. (2001) *Bridget Jones's Diary.* London: The Independent Newspaper.

FORBES MAGAZINE, (2020) *Are You Getting Enough Hugs?* New Jersey: Forbes Magazine.

FRANKL, V.E. (2004) *Man's Search for Meaning.* London: Rider Books.

GERMER, C. (2009) The *Mindful Path to Self-Compassion: Freeing Yourself From Destructive Thoughts and Emotions.* London: Guildford Press.

GILBERT, P. (2013) *The Compassionate Mind.* London: Constable and Robinson.

GOLEMAN, D. (1996) *Emotional Intelligence: Why it can matter more than IQ.* London: Bloomsbury Publishing PLC.

GOLEMAN, D.; DAVIDSON, R. (2017) *Altered Traits: Science Reveals How Meditation Changes Your Mind, Brain and Body.* Massachusetts: More than Sound LLC.

HANSON, R. (2009) *Buddha's Brain.* California: New Harbinger Publications.

HANSON, R. (2014) *Hardwiring Happiness.* London: Ebury Publishing.

HAWKINS, D. (2006) *Power vs Force: The Hidden Determinants of Human Behaviour.* Arizona: Veritas Publishing.

HAWKINS, D. (2013) *Transcending the Levels of Consciousness: The Stairway to Enlightenment.* California: Hay House LLC.

HEWETT, M. (2020) *Meant for More: Stop Struggling and Become A Force to Be Reckoned With.* Audible: Mia Hewett.

HOWARD, A. (2023) *It's Not Your Fault: Why Childhood Trauma Shapes You and How to Break Free.* Audible: Hay House UK.

HEALTH EDITORIAL TEAM (2020) *What are Stress and Anxiety?* Online: Healthline.com https://www.healthline.com/health/stress-and-anxiety Accessed: May 2021.

HEALTHLINE.COM (2018) *Emotional Signs of Too Much Stress.* Online: https://www.healthline.com/health/emotional-symptoms-of-stress-depression. Accessed: March 2021.

HEALTHLINE.COM (2020) *Glucocorticoids: List, Uses, Side Effects, and More.* Online: https://www.healthline.com › health › glucocorticoids. Accessed June 2021.

HEBB, D. (1949) & (2002) *The Organisation of Behaviour.* New York: Psychology Press.

HEALTH AND SAFETY EXECUTIVE, (2019) *Work-related stress, anxiety or depression statistics in Great Britain, 2019*. Online: Health and Safety Executive. https://www.hse.gov.uk/statistics/causdis/stress.pdf Accessed: October 2020.

HEALTH AND SAFETY EXECUTIVE, (2020) *Work-related stress, anxiety or depression statistics in Great Britain, 2020.* Online: Health and Safety Executive. https://www.hse.gov.uk/statistics/causdis/stress.pdf. Accessed June 2021.

HISTORIC LIVERPOOL (2025) *History of Speke: the coming to and leaving of Liverpool.* Online: https://historic-liverpool.co.uk/historic-townships/speke/. Accessed March 2025.

HOLIDAY, R. (2016) *Ego is the Enemy: The Fight to Master Our Greatest Opponent*. London: Profile Books Ltd.

HURLEY, K. (2020) *Stress vs Anxiety: How to Tell the Difference.* Online: Psycom.net https://www.psycom.net/stress-vs-anxiety-difference Accessed: November 2020

KABAT-ZINN, J. (1994) *Wherever You Go There You Are.* London: Paiktus, Little Brown Book Group, Kindle edition.

KABAT-ZINN, J. (2015) *Full Catastrophe Living, Using the Wisdom of Your Body and Mind to Face Stress, Pain and Illness.* Published by Audible: 15th Anniversary Audio Book Edition.

LIPTON, B., CHATTERGEE, R. (2023) *How To Reprogram Your Mind While You Sleep To Heal The Body & Mind.* Online YouTube: https://www.youtube.com/watch?v=gjcud_y9w9u. Accessed January 2025.

MARK, J. J. (2014) *The World's Oldest Love Poem.* Online: World History Encyclopaedia. https://www.worldhistory.org/article/750/the-worlds-oldest-love-poem. Accessed March 2025.

MASLO, A. (1943) *A Theory of Human Motivation.* Unknown: Motivation & Personality Journal.

MATÉ, G. (2003) *When the Body Says No: The Cost of Hidden Stress.* Audible: Penguin Audio

MCKUSICK, E. (2021) *Electric Body, Electric Health.* Audible: McMillan Audio.

NAGY, K. (2022) *A Guide to the 12 Major Meridians of the Body.* Online: Remedy Grove. https://remedygrove.com/traditional/The-Guide-To-The-12-Major-Meridians-of-the-Body. Accessed April 2025.

NAIRN, R. (1999) *Diamond Mind: A Psychology of Meditation.* Boston: Shambhala.

NEFF, C. (2011) *Self Compassion – stop beating yourself up and leave insecurity behind.* London: Hodder and Stoughton.

NEUROLAUNCH.COM (2024) *Confusion: Unravelling Its Role in Human Emotions.* Online: https://neurolaunch.com/is-confusion-an-emotion. Accessed January 2024.

NHAT-HANH, T. (1998) *Mindfulness & Psychotherapy: Working with Anger and Nourishing Inner Peace Each and Every Day – Especially for Psychotherapists.* Colorado: Sounds True. Edition: Audio CD.

OLYPHANT, T. (2004) Is the Juice Worth the Squeeze? And Other Familiar Catchphrases. Online: Medium.Com. https://medium.com/the-orange-journal/is-the-juice-worth-the-squeeze-and-other-familiar-catchphrases -69f3e2ddb36b/. Accessed March 2025.

PORGES, S. (2011) *The Polyvagal Theory: Neurophysiological Foundations of Emotions, Attachment, Communication and Self-Regulation.* New York: WW Norton.

PURSER, R. (2019) *McMindfulness: How Mindfulness Became the New Capitalist Spirituality.* London: Repeater.

RINPOCHE, T.; SWANSON, E. (2012) *Open Heart, Open Mind. A Guide To Inner Transformation.* London: Rider.

RIZVI (2025) *Quantum Manifestation: The Science of Abundance.* Online: Insight Timer.

ROBBINS, T. (2020) *Unleash the Power Within, Personal Coaching to Transform Your Life.* Audio: Simon & Schuster Audio.

SAPOLSKY, R. (2012) *Why Zebras Don't Get Ulcers: The Acclaimed Guide to Stress, Stress-Related Diseases, and Coping.* Audiobook: Tantor Audio.

SATIR, V. (1991) *The Satir Model: Family Therapy and Beyond.* California: Science and Behaviour Books.

SEGAL, Z.V.; WILLIAMS, J.M.G.; TEASDALE, J.D. (2002) *Mindfulness-Based Cognitive Therapy for Depression: A new approach to preventing relapse.* New York: Guilford.

SEGAL, Z.V.; WILLIAMS, J.M.G.; TEASDALE, J.D. (2012) *Mindfulness-Based Cognitive Therapy for Depression.* London: Guilford Press.

SELYE, H. (1956) *The stress of life.* New York: McGraw-Hill.

SIEGAL, D. J. (2011) *Mindsight: The New Science of Personal Transformation.* New York: Bantam Books.

SINEK, S. (2009) Start With *Why: How Great Leaders Inspire Everyone to Take Action.* Audio: Penguin Audio.

SISNEY, L. (2023) *Organizational Physics: The Science of Growing A Business.* Audible: Organizational Physics Inc.

SLATER & GORDON (2014) *Workplace Stress: A Stigma in the UK.* Online: https://www.slatergordon.co.uk/media-centre/press-releases/2014/07/workplace-stress-a-stigma-in-uk/ Accessed: March 2020.

SMAIL, D. (2015) *Illusion and Reality: The Meaning of Anxiety.* London: Karmac Books.

TAN, C.M. (2014) *Search Inside Yourself: The Unexpected Path to Achieving Success, Happiness (and World Peace).* New York: Harper Collins.

THOUGHTCO.COM (2024), *How Fast Does the Earth Spin?* Online: Thoughtco.com. Accessed: March 2025. https://www.thoughtco.com/speed-of-the-earth-1435093

TOLLE, E. (2001) *The Power of Now: A Guide to Spiritual Enlightenment.* London: Hodder & Stoughton.

TOLLE, E. (2004) *A New Earth: Awakening Your Life's Purpose.* Audible: Penguin Audio.

TOLLE, E. (2011) *Freedom from the World.* Audible: Eckhart Teachings.

WALLACE, A.B. (2007) *Contemplative Science: Where Buddhism and Neuroscience Converge.* New York: Columbia University Press.

WAX, R. (2013) *Sane New World.* London: Hodder & Stoughton.

WAX, R. (2018) *How to be Human.* London: Penguin Random House UK.

WELTI, P. (2020) *The Dandelion's Fall From Grace Has Been a Doozy. Can this Weed Become A Flower Again?* Online: Science & Nature. https://news.wttw.com/2020/05/14/dandelion-weed-flower-history. Accessed March 2025.

WHO (2001) *Mental Disorders Affect One in Four People.* Online: https://www.who.int/whr/2001/media_centre/press_release/en/ Accessed: November 2018.

WHO (2019) *Burn-out an "occupational phenomenon": International Classification of Diseases.* Online: https://www.who.int/mental_health/evidence/burn-out/en/ Accessed: October 2020.

WIKIPEDIA (2005) *Kinesiology* Online: https://en.wikipedia.org/wiki/kinesiology. Accessed April 2025.

WILLIAMS, M.; TEASDALE, J.; SEGAL, Z.; KABAT-ZINN, J. (2007) *The Mindful Way Through Depression: Freeing Yourself from Chronic Unhappiness.* New York: Guilford Press.

YOURHORMONES.INFO (Undated), *You and your hormones: cortisol.* Online: https://www.yourhormones.info/hormones/cortisol/. Accessed May 2021.

VAN DER KOLK, B. (2015) *The Body Keeps the Score: Mind, Brain and Body in the Transformation of Trauma.* London: Penguin.

Acknowledgements

To my husband, Mike, for his ongoing encouragement in the face of my many doubts. Thank you for spurring me on, feeding me and for providing all of those writer's treats. It turns out you were right! It wasn't just a little book.

I couldn't have done this without the support of my family and friends, many of whom have been listening to me talk about my book for nearly five years.

A special thank you to my friend Helen, my proofreader and cheerleader. Your feedback on that sample chapter had a profound impact on my writing style. Without it, the book would be technically correct but possibly a little boring. I'm forever grateful for your help and support. Thank you to Lou for posing as my ideal reader. It was so kind of you to allow me to interview you in Poyser's patch. What a treat.

It's been an absolute pleasure to work alongside Estelle Maher and her amazing team at TAUK Publishing. Thank you for all of those commas and for reminding me that penguins can't actually fly!

Thank you, Heather Regan-Addis, for not allowing me to hide during my first year at university. Your kindness helped me through some very difficult times. Learning to teach mindfulness has been life changing. I wouldn't have qualified without the direction from two excellent teachers, Heather and Choden. I'd also like to thank Colette Savage, another great lecturer. Thank you for getting me through that dissertation, most of which I think I've rehashed and put in the book, but don't tell anyone.

Thank you to all of those people who allowed me to practice on them before I gained my qualifications, Frank, Kerry, Alison, Shaun, Julie, Clare, Kelly, Tasha, Catherine and the secret meditation group at Very. A huge thank you to all of the lovely customers who have worked with me over the past five years.

Each and every one of those experiences have helped to bring this book to fruition.

About the Author

Julie Perrigo is a mindfulness teacher, author, and former corporate IT warrior who swapped servers and spreadsheets for stillness and self-discovery. With a master's degree in mindfulness and another in Information Technology (because, why not?), Julie brings a refreshingly down-to-earth approach to personal transformation. After years in the fast-paced tech world left her feeling disconnected and overwhelmed, Julie took a deep breath, literally, and began a journey inward. Mindfulness helped her unpack a lifetime's worth of emotional baggage and completely reshape her life. Now, from her cosy home on the windswept Wirral coast in North West England, she's on a mission to help others do the same.

This is her first book, written with heart, humour, and a genuine desire to help people live more meaningful, joy-filled lives. She's poured everything she's learned (and a bit of herself) into these pages. So settle in, take a breath, and get ready to feel inspired.

Social Media Links

Instagram - @theemotionalhustle
YouTube - @JuliePerrigo-EmotionalHustle

For help and support, the practices discussed in this book are available via our membership program, which can be accessed at:

www.justbreathesolutions.co.uk/emotional-hustle

Printed in Dunstable, United Kingdom

66331803R10171